THE BRIDGESTONE

100 BEST

RESTAURANTS & PLACES TO STAY IN IRELAND

'96

JOHN & SALLY McKENNA

FIRST PUBLISHED IN JUNE 1996 BY ESTRAGON PRESS

REPRINTED JUNE 1996

© ESTRAGON PRESS

TEXT © JOHN AND SALLY McKENNA

THE MORAL RIGHT OF THE AUTHORS HAS BEEN ASSERTED

ISBN 1 874076 18 9

DESIGNED BY NICK CANN

COVER ILLUSTRATION BY MICHAEL FRITH

MAP ILLUSTRATED BY WENDY ROBINSON

PRINTED BY COLOUR BOOKS LTD

FOR RAY AND JO BUCKLEY

WITH THANKS TO:

Des Collins, Colm Conyngham, Eddie, Nick Cann, Pat Young,
Caroline McGrath, Denis Cotter, Maureen Daly, Colette Tobin,
Paula, Kevin and Ana, Pat Ruane, Margie, Lelia, Belinda, Martin,
Jakki and Maurice

JOHN McKENNA was born in Belfast and educated there and in Dublin, where
he practised as a barrister before turning to writing in 1989. He has won three
Glenfiddich Awards, as Regional Writer, Radio Broadcaster and Restaurant Writer,
in 1993, 1994 and 1995.

SALLY McKENNA was born in Kenya, and brought up on the Pacific island of Fiji
before coming to Ireland in 1982. She cooked professionally before turning to
writing about cookery and food.

■ John and Sally write and present the RTE television programme
McKENNAS' IRELAND. They live in Cork with their children Connie and Sam.

CONTENTS

HOW TO USE THIS BOOK

This book is arranged **ALPHABETI-CALLY**, firstly into the four provinces of Ireland – Connaught, Leinster, Munster and Ulster – and then into the individual counties within the provinces. Within the counties, the arrangement of the entries again follow alphabetically.

■ Entries in Northern Ireland, though part of the Ulster section, are itemised at the end of the book.

■ The contents of the Bridgestone 100 Best Guide are exclusively the result of the authors' deliberations. All meals and accommodation were paid for and any offers of discounts or gifts were refused.

■ In a number of cases, where we have encountered a restaurateur or hotelier whose work represents a special and unique effort in terms of Irish food, we have awarded these people a star and marked these entries thus: ✪
These people are, simply, the very best at what they do.

■ In other cases where we felt the food was of special interest we have marked the entry with a ➔, meaning that the entry is worthy of making a special detour to enjoy the food.

■ Many of the Country Houses and B&Bs featured in this book are only open during the summer season, which means that they can be closed for any given length of time between October and March. Many others change their opening times during the winter. Even though opening times are given for restaurants it is always advisable in Ireland to telephone in advance and check opening times when booking.

PRICES All prices and details are correct at the time of going to press. Should the circumstances of any of the entries change, however, we are unable to accept any responsibility.

■ Finally, we greatly appreciate receiving reports, suggestions and criticisms from readers, and would like to thank those who have written in the past, whose opinions are of enormous assistance to us.

KEY: **Restaurant** Ⓡ   **Accommodation**

BRIDGESTONE

BRIDGESTONE is Japan's largest tyre manufacturer and the world's largest producer of rubber products.

Founded in 1931, it currently employs over 95,000 people in Europe, Asia and America and its products are sold in more than 150 countries. Its European plants are situated in France, Spain and Italy.

■ Bridgestone manufacture tyres for a wide variety of vehicles from passenger cars and motorcycles, trucks and buses to giant earthmovers and aircraft.

■ Many Japanese cars sold in Ireland have been fitted with Bridgestone tyres during manufacture and a host of exotic sports cars including Ferrari, Lamborghini, Porsche and Jaguar are fitted with Bridgestone performance tyres as original equipment.

■ Bridgestone commercial vehicle tyres enjoy a worldwide reputation for superior cost per kilometre performance and its aircraft tyres are used by more than 100 airlines.

■ In 1988 Bridgestone acquired the Firestone Tyre and Rubber Company combining the resources of both companies under one umbrella. This cou-

pled with an intensive research and development programme has enabled Bridgestone to remain the world's most technologically advanced tyre company with testing centres in Japan, USA, Mexico and Italy.

■ Bridgestone tyres are distributed in Ireland by Bridgestone/Firestone Ireland Limited, a subsidiary of the multinational Bridgestone Corporation. A wide range of tyres are stocked in its central warehouse and staff provide sales, technical and delivery services all over the country.

■ Bridgestone tyres are available from tyre dealers throughout Ireland.

For further information:
BRIDGESTONE/FIRESTONE IRELAND LTD
Unit 4
Leopardstown Office Park,
Dublin 18
Tel: (01) 295 2844
Fax: (01) 295 2858

34 Hillsborough Road,
Lisburn
BT28 1AQ
Tel: (01 846) 678331
Fax: (01 846) 673235

THE BRIDGESTONE AWARDS

✪ BRIDGESTONE AWARD - THE VERY BEST
➔ WORTHY OF A DETOUR

CONNAUGHT
County Galway
✪ Drimcong House
Moycullen
Gerry & Marie Galvin

✪ Erriseaske House Hotel
Ballyconneely
The Matz Brothers

➔ Kille House, Clifden
Anya Brand Vermoolen

✪ Norman Villa, Galway
Dee & Mark Keogh

County Sligo
✪ Temple House
Ballymote
Sandy & Deb Perceval

✪ Truffles, Sligo
Bernadette O'Shea

LEINSTER
County Dublin
➔ Chestnut Lodge
Monkstown
Nancy Malone

✪ L'Ecrivain, Dublin 2
Derry & Sally-Anne Clarke

➔ Number 31, Dublin 2
Brian & Mary Bennett

✪ Peacock Alley, Dublin 2
Conrad Gallagher

✪ Thornton's, Dublin 8
Kevin Thornton

County Kildare
➔ Tonlegee House, Athy
Mark & Marjorie Molloy

County Kilkenny
✪ Lacken House, Kilkenny
Eugene & Breda McSweeney

MUNSTER
County Cork
✪ Adele's, Schull
Adele & Simon Connor

✪ Assolas House, Kanturk
Joe & Hazel Bourke

✪ Clifford's
Cork City
Michael & Deirdre Clifford

➔ Dunworley Cottage
Butlerstown
Katherine Noren

➔ Heir Island Restaurant
Skibbereen
John Desmond & Ellmary
Fenton

➔ The Ivory Tower
Cork City
Seamus O'Connell

➔ Lettercollum House
Timoleague
Con McLoughlin & Karen
Austin

✪ Longueville House
Mallow
William & Aisling
O'Callaghan

✪ The Oystercatcher
Oysterhaven
Bill & Sylvia Patterson

➔ Seven North Mall, Cork
Angela Hegarty

County Kerry
➔ Loaves and Fishes
Caherdaniel
Helen Mullane & Armel
Whyte

➔ Packie's
Kenmare
Maura Foley

County Limerick
➔ Echo Lodge
Ballingarry
Dan Mullane

ULSTER
County Monaghan
✪ Hilton Park
Scotshouse
Johnny & Lucy Madden

NORTHERN IRELAND
County Antrim
➔ Nick's Warehouse
Belfast
Nick & Cathy Price

➔ The Sun Kee
Belfast
Edmond Lau

✪ Roscoff
Belfast
Paul & Jeanne Rankin

County Down
✪ Shanks
Bangor
Robbie & Shirley Millar

County Londonderry
✪ Beech Hill Hotel
Derry
Noel McMeel

These are the 100 Best places to eat, and to stay, in Ireland.

They have been chosen for the spontaniety of their hospitality, the creativity of their cooking, and the sense of genuine character which they create.

Any book of this nature must, of course, leave out many establishments which are excellent and accomplished.

But we hope, nevertheless, that these 100 best offer a range of places to suit all people and all pockets.

Some of them may appear somewhat unlikely, some of them may appear distinctly unlikely, but we believe that these 100 places, and the people who run them, are those addresses which are currently the most exciting, and the most enjoyable, to be found throughout Ireland.

JOHN AND SALLY MCKENNA
DURRUS,
COUNTY CORK

CONNAUGHT

the West's awakening

DESTRY'S ®
**Paddy Foyle, Dermot Gannon
The Square
Clifden
Connemara
Co Galway
Tel: (095) 21722**

It was Lord Beaverbrook, no less, who said that the sight of Marlene Dietrich, standing on a bar, wearing black net stockings and belting out "See What The Boys In The Back Room Will Have", in the classic movie "Destry Rides Again", was a greater work of art than the Venus de Milo.

His lordship may very well have been right, but what is certain, for sure, is that whilst Marlene may be the greater work of art, Venus is, beyond question, the better singer.

Paddy Foyle's admiration of Marlene has extended not just to borrowing the title from the droll, ironic western in which she starred with James Stewart, but has extended also to borrowing some of the lady's capacity for re-invention. It was a desire to simplify his food, and to work in a funkier ambience, which led to the creation of this splendid place, not too far from his original stomping ground of Rosleague Manor, and just up the hill from his most recent invention, the splendid Quay House.

Destry's is a restaurant which gallops along on good humour, good food – this the work of a modest and super-talented young man, Dermot Gannon – and that adrenalinated, holiday-town energy which gives such distinction to Clifden.

The cooking enjoys Mr Foyle's signature, that intuitive grasp for motivating flavour in a dish and finding unusual alliances, and Mr Gannon understands the imprimatur of his mentor. The marinated leg of lamb may seem as untypical an Irish dish as you could imagine – the cubes of meat are char-grilled to a rich spiciness and offset by a chutney sauce – but the flavours in each and every dish could be found nowhere else than the west coast of ireland.

There are clever experiments to enjoy, such as coating white hake in black sesame seeds to produce a dish that dazzles both vision and appetite, but Dermot Gannon never loses the logic of a dish, which means his food is deeply enjoyable.

Clifden has needed a place like Destry for a long time: someplace to enjoy 5 Star fish 'n' chips, that perfect somewhere that matches the exuberance of the holidaymaker, somewhere kids just adore, somewhere that pulses with the pleasure of good food and good times.

● **OPEN:** Noon-3.30pm, 6.30-9.30pm Tue-Sun. (Closed Nov-mid-Mar).
● **AVERAGE PRICE:** Lunch £7.
À la carte Dinner from £12.50.
House Wine £12.
No Service Charge.
● **CREDIT CARDS:**
Visa, Access/Master.

● **NOTES:**
Wine Licence.
Wheelchair Access.
Children – always welcome, menus by arrangement.
Clifden town centre.

DRIMCONG HOUSE ®✪
Gerry & Marie Galvin
Moycullen
Co Galway
Tel: (091) 85115

"My motivation and my guiding light is to experiment and, being Irish, to try to build on what we have", writes Gerry Galvin in his marvellous book of recipes, recollections and poems, "The Drimcong Food Affair".

Mr Galvin, happily, is a man of action as much as a man of words and, if he is one of the leading intellects and thinkers in the world of Irish food, he is also one of its principal practical exponents.

His experiments are creative and continuous, with each weekly menu drawing new ideas from the chef himself and his team. Typical of the man is the fact that Drimcong has begun over the years to establish itself as a superb training ground for young cooks, and a plenitude of youngsters has emerged from under Mr Galvin's wings to carry off cooking awards and to begin to establish themselves as serious individuals. Teacher as well as preacher.

His dish of black pudding and oysters with an apple and onion confit is already a legend, and he will improvise it into a marvellous black pudding mousse, or a startling black and white pudding terrine. This touch with rustic, obvious foods, this attempt to heighten and isolate flavours, is found in creations such as the Connemara lamb with a mousse of peas and a garlic gravy, in

pigeon with couscous and a red wine sauce, in a rabbit and venison pie with a chocolate flavoured sauce, in simple things such as colcannon soup, tipsy pudding, roast pike.

There are marvellous foods for vegetarians – herb and parmesan omelette, polenta and aubergine gâteau – and splendid, real food for children – pan-fried chicken or grilled fish, zippy ice-creams. But, whatever one chooses, certain truths emerge about the cooking: it is deeply considered, truly generous in spirit, is motivated by a hungry creativity, and it is distinctly, creatively Irish. Drimcong House, with its splendid staff and their obvious happiness and pride in their work, its aura of serenity and its respect for the efforts of those who work here and those who eat here, is a magnificent creation.

● **OPEN:** 6.30pm-10.30pm Tue-Sat. (Closed Xmas-Mar).
● **AVERAGE PRICE:** Table d'hôte Dinner £24. House wine £10.50. No Service Charge.
● **CREDIT CARDS:**
Visa, Access/Master, Amex, Diners.

● **NOTES:**
Full Licence.
Wheelchair Access (apart from three negotiable steps to hall).
Children – high chairs, children's menu £9.50.
Recommended for Vegetarians – special menu £19.50.
Driving on the N59 out of Galway to Clifden, a few miles west of Moycullen, the restaurant is signposted on the right hand side.

ERRISEASKE HOUSE HOTEL & RESTAURANT ◓◒✦

Christian & Stefan Matz
Ballyconneely, Clifden
Co Galway
Tel: (095) 23553 Fax: 23639

For very many people, Stefan Matz's cooking in the Erriseaske is the finest they have enjoyed in Ireland.

What bedazzles people so? Probably, more than anything else, it is Stefan Matz's ability to use all his skills to make something deliciously effective, for here is a virtuoso who orchestrates his skills in service to the melody of great cooking.

When you enjoy a bowl of his perfect tomato consommé, for example, or his magret of duck with homemade noodles, or a savarin of salmon, you don't have a mind to the stupendously protracted preparation needed to make these dishes. All you can think of is how sensational, subtle, seductive this cooking is.

This is Mr Matz's gift. The hard work of culinary preparation is hidden in his cooking. His immense pyrotechnical skills are subjugated in the cause of flavour.

When you try his veal parcel, the carefully sourced and humanely reared meat wrapped in pastry with glazed sweetbreads, or a knockout dish of loin of Connemara lamb with a jus of fresh thyme, you don't ooh! and aah! over the arrangement of the plate or the display of colour. What you ooh! and aah! over is the flavour and the success of the dish as a whole, the ability of the flavours to intoxicate and entrance you.

His skill is evident right throughout a meal: from a terrific soup of watercress with fish julienne, a main course of his intricately elaborate ravioli, a dessert of lemon tart with a pastry that is nothing less than ethereal. This is cookery built around essentials and essences. The essential things are assembled on the plate to make the dish work. The essences are the pure flavours which Stefan Matz extracts from each ingredient

Modesty and a lack of display are major factors of the success of the Erriseaske. It is a small, quiet restaurant – some say too quiet – with rooms in a lonely and lovely spot on the coastline, and so the world-class nature of the cooking comes almost as a shock.

But that it is world class cooking is undoubted: dinner in Erriseaske can be a starburst of brilliance, with the flavour and sensitivity of every dish precisely, perfectly realised.

- **OPEN:** 1pm-2pm Thur-Tue, 6.30pm-9pm Mon-Sun. (Closed Nov-Apr).
- **ROOMS:** Thirteen, all en suite.
- **AVERAGE PRICE:** B&B £30-£50 per person sharing. Residents Dinner £17.90. Table d'hôte Dinner £23.50. House Wine from £11. No Service Charge.
- **CREDIT CARDS:**
Visa, Access/Master, Amex, Diners.

- **NOTES:**
Restaurant Licence.
No Wheelchair Access.
Children – high chairs.
Restaurant booking for non residents advised.
Take the coast road from Clifden to Ballyconneely, then follow the signposts.

KILLE HOUSE 🔷➡️
Anya Brand Vermoolen
Kingstown, Clifden, Co Galway
Tel: (095) 21849

We are indebted to Francis Rochford and Mary Daly for the following story about Kille House.

Early in the century, it was owned by a local cleric who, in the manner of clerics both local and international, was rather too fond of the drink. The happy tippler eventually ran up a tab of £25 with the local publican. Unable to settle his slate, he handed the pub owner the keys of the house. Most intriguingly, say Mr Rochford and Ms Daly, this cleric had the delightful habit, when jarred, of playing his piano in the nude.

We have to confess that we were rather too shy to ask Anya Vermoolen if the habits of the former owner of the house were still practiced today, but we suspect it is unlikely, for Kille is a house of pristine elegance, and even a cleric might feel it was not the proper place to try to be a deshabillé Jelly Roll Morton.

This is not to suggest that it is even slightly stuffy or dull, however. Far from it. This is a fun house, distinguished by housekeeping of such an extraordinary standard that there are few other places in the country to which it can be compared. You fold yourself into a big, snowy-white duvet in a big beautiful bed in a big handsome room after a big long soak in a big big bath and thank the stars you are in Connemara, and here in Kille, with

the promise of a fine breakfast –softly toothsome meat loaf, splendid salamis, good eggs, fine cheeses, crumbly, warm bread and excellent coffee – to shake you into shape in the morning.

We regret to inform clerics that we have no plans, at the present, to write "The 100 Best Places In Which to Play Piano in the Nude in Ireland".

● **OPEN:** Apr-Oct.
● **ROOMS:** Four rooms, two en suite, two sharing 1 bathroom.
● **AVERAGE PRICE:** B&B £20-£25 per person sharing. Set Dinner £17. No Service Charge.
● **CREDIT CARDS:** No Credit Cards.

● **NOTES:**
No Drinks Licence.
Dinner for guests only, book by noon.
No Wheelchair Access.
Children – on request.
No pets.
In Clifden, take the Sky Road, and from this you will see the small hand-written sign directing you to the house.

MOYCULLEN HOUSE 🔷
Philip & Marie Casburn
Moycullen, Co Galway
Tel: (091) 85566

Moycullen is one of those houses that offers the peace of familiarity and the assurance of fond memories each and every time you return to it.

Like a gin and tonic at six o'clock, or marmalade on your toast at breakfast, it is nothing new, but something you always want, something that is enduringly, endearingly, enjoyable.

Partly this is thanks to the house itself. An old sporting lodge built for wild west of Ireland weekends, it is unpretentious, cosy, an affable place. Architecturally it is a rarity in Ireland, set precisely in the Arts and Crafts style, a design which allows it to seem quaint yet proud, and which evokes visions of GBS in his tweeds, or Cary Grant in something smarter, sitting in the lounge reading yesterday's papers.

But it is Philip and Marie Casburn themselves who provide the core of Moycullen's soft, hazy, lazy air. Their easy ease, and Marie's unflustered comfort cooking, are as essential a part of Moycullen as the antique baths, the cushiony carpets, the cranky furniture, the buckets of fresh air, the lovely gardens.

Everything in the house, from the beds with their soft creakiness, to the gripping comfort of the chairs, to the succulence of mashed spuds with roast lamb, preceded by kidneys in a sherry sauce and followed by a big creamy gateau, seems to knock the pent-up stuffing out of you, leaving you wanting more and more of this graceful, naïve, house.

● **OPEN:** Mar-Nov.
● **ROOMS:** Five double bedrooms, each with private bath.
● **AVERAGE PRICE:** £30 per person sharing.
Dinner £18. No Service Charge.
● **CREDIT CARDS:** Visa, Access/Master

● **NOTES:**
Dinner for residents only, 7pm.

No Drinks Licence. Bring Your Own.
No Wheelchair Access.
Children – welcome. No pets.
Moycullen House is off the N59.
Turn left in Moycullen village, taking the Spiddal road, drive up the hill until you see the sign for the house.

TIGH NEACHTAIN RESTAURANT ✪
Stephan & Maureen Zeltner-Healy
Quay Street
Galway
Co Galway
Tel: (091) 566172/546403

Perhaps the best way to make your way upstairs to the restaurant in Neachtain's is to arrive through the main part of one of Galway's most authentic pubs. Tigh Neachtain, in this delightedly frisky part of town known as Galway's "Latin Quarter", is famous not only for good pints but also for good music. It is now, happily, getting a name for good food.

This is thanks to Stephan and Maureen Zeltner-Healy. He is the chef, and she is always to be found front of house, amidst the burgundy walls, the open fires and the candle light.

Curiously, for somewhere over a pub, Neachtain's has a sort of Country House Parlour atmosphere. It's not very formal: nobody bothers whispering in here, so it's a good place to pick up hot Galway gossip.

There is a table d'hôte, an à la carte and – the most adventurous – a

Stephan Special, and they all share excellent value for money.

Mr Zeltner-Healy makes a fine oyster and mussel ragout – sweet seafood in a sauce flavoured with dried mushrooms – and grills marinated lemon sole which is served on top of good lettuce leaves.

His fondness for profound, punchy flavours is best seen in main courses, like grilled loin of venison which comes with a rich date and honey sauce, or roast breast of Barbary duck which is knocked into compliance by a powerful boletus sauce. Vegetables are good, and properly served: no dread kidney plates.

Puddings are enjoyably classical: syrupy pears poached in red wine with a brandy parfait; some tangy stewed berries with mixed parfaits. The wine list is decent and decently priced, and Galway is richer for having this alliance of good food and great crack, this careful, appropriate respect for good cooking and good hospitality.

● **OPEN:** 7pm-10.30pm Tue-Sat.
(Closed 2 weeks in Sept).
● **AVERAGE PRICE:** Dinner £17-£22.75.
House Wine £10.50.
No Service Charge.
● **CREDIT CARDS:**
Visa, Access/Master.

● **NOTES:**
Full Licence.
No Wheelchair Access.
Children – over 5yrs welcome.
Vegetarian menu always available £15.50.
On the corner of Cross Street and Quay Street, in the centre of Galway city.

NORMAN VILLA ◎ ✪
Dee & Mark Keogh
86 Lower Salthill,
Co Galway
Tel: (091) 521131

It is fun to be in Norman Villa, fun to find yourself here, fun to wrap yourself in the embrace of such a pristine, perfect B&B.

And it is fun to meet Mark and Dee Keogh, and fun to enjoy their vivacious, spontaneous hospitality. My goodness, whenever did you last have so much fun?

But this is the secret of Norman Villa. In anyone else's hands, a house of such cool, mannered design would risk becoming precious, fey, self-regarding. The Keoghs, however, are able to take the mickey out of their obsession with design, are able to create a space which they enjoy, rather than merely admire.

And whilst you will admire the house – the cool glade of the entrance hall, the symphony of style which graces the bedrooms, the perfectly understood composure of the breakfast room – you will, above all else, enjoy it. Only in Galway, with its fiercely libertine sense of indulgence and its spiffing sense of style, could you find a place like this.

In many ways, Mark and Dee regard Norman Villa as a creative space and, like artists, they ceaselessly apply and erase, apply and erase. The first time you visit the house, its strong sense of order will seem nothing less than perfect.

But when you return, and some additions and improvements have been made, some refinements and variations, then you find yourself saying "Of course, of course!". Each effort by the Keoghs tries to uncover some other aspect, some other side, of the house. It is a fascinating experiment, a fascinating labour of love, and even as a mere guest you become absorbed in this dazzling exercise of theme and variations.

- **OPEN:** All year
(except two weeks in Jan)
- **ROOMS:** Five rooms, all en suite
- **AVERAGE PRICE:** B&B £22 per person sharing, £30 single.
- **CREDIT CARDS:** Visa, Access/Master.

- **NOTES:**
Open for Xmas.
No restaurant, apart from Xmas.
No Wheelchair Access.
£2 surcharge on summer bank holidays and racing weekends.
Children – 25% discount.
No pets.
One mile from Galway city centre, follow signs for Lower Salthill, and the house is 500 yards from Claddagh Palace Cinema.

THE QUAY HOUSE
Paddy & Julia Foyle
Clifden, Co Galway
Tel: (095) 21369

The Quay House, a handsome big pile which peers right out over the harbour front in Clifden, exploits to the full Paddy and Julia Foyle's desire to avoid the obvious, their enjoyment of the ironic interplay and counterpoint between fixtures and furnishings in a room.

In short, Mr and Mrs Foyle have given birth to a masterpiece, and staying in Quay House is one of the great delights of Ireland.

The design, from bedrooms to dining room, is quite wondrous. An eclectic mixing of solid family furniture, "found" objects, gilt-framed dark Victorian paintings, shuttered windows with bright checked curtains, Lloyd loom chairs, a corridor with an avenue of deer heads and the massive skin of a tiger which, in its time, had eaten seven Indian women, it is splendidly rich and amusing.

Throughout, the house wears the stamp of Paddy Foyle's individual style. He has said that it is very important for him that his work should be different from the way others do things, but Quay House shows hat in avoiding the obvious, he also never makes the mistake of tumbling into self-consciousness. This is a darling, carefree place, which feels like it has been here for ever, and makes you want to stay that long.

- **OPEN:** Mid Mar-Nov.
- **ROOMS:** Eight, all en suite.
- **AVERAGE PRICE:** £30-£35 per person sharing.
No Service Charge.
- **CREDIT CARDS:** Visa, Access/Master.
- **DINNER:** From 7.30pm-9.30pm. Table d'hôte £20. House wines £12.50

- **NOTES:**
Dinner for non residents if pre-booked.
Wine Licence.
Wheelchair Access.
Children – welcome, but no facilities.
Down on the quay in Clifden.

ECHOES ®
Siobhan, Tom & Helen Ryan
Main Street
Cong
Co Mayo
Tel: (092) 46059

Whilst Siobhan Ryan garners most of the attention in Echoes – quite rightly, for she is the person who devises the dishes and is the instrumental force in getting them from stove to table – she could not do so without her Dad, who takes care of all manner of supplies to the restaurant, and young Tom, the brother, who is not only an award-winning butcher, but also not above hopping into the kitchen to rattle the pots and pans when Siobhan takes a deserved break.

Siobhan's sister brings to the job of waiting on table a feline grace and a skill which turns her work into an art form. Finally, Siobhan's mother, who welcomes you, organises the bills and cooks breakfast in the restaurant during the summer months, completes this extra-ordinary picture. It's a family affair.

Together, the family all work to the benefit of the fine food you can expect in Echoes: home-smoked wild salmon on top of a springy bed of crisp salad leaves; breaded monkfish between slabs of green bacon and onions and peppers; fat scallops in a mornay sauce served on the shell surrounded by piped potato; sweet mountain lamb; ice-creams which are the stuff you scream for in your dreams.

At some time in the future some-one, with enough time on their hands, will sit down and count the number of times the superlative "Excellent!" – always accompanied by an exclamation mark – appears in the visitors' book to describe Siobhan Ryan's cooking.

Amidst the endless parade of "Excellents!" there appears the heart-felt plea: "Could you post me the recipe for brown bread ice cream?". If you can resist that as a recommendation, then you are made of stern stuff. Those made of less stern stuff will simply melt with joy at this cool, boozy dessert.

This deeply comforting food, full of odoriferous scents and rich with goodness, comes in grandly generous portions, and the happy family affair of Echoes is as far removed from the self-conscious sense of denial that pervades so much of Mayo and the Mayo mentality as you could possibly imagine.

● **OPEN:** Noon-2.30pm,
6.30pm-10pm Mon-Sun.
(Shorter hours during winter season).
● **AVERAGE PRICE:**
À la carte Lunch £7-£14.
À la carte Dinner £19.
House Wine £9.50.
No Service Charge.
● **CREDIT CARDS:**
Visa, Access/Master, Amex.

● **NOTES:**
Wine Licence.
Wheelchair Access.
Children – high chairs and special menus.
Vegetarian options always available.
Echoes is right in the centre of Cong village, next to the butcher's shop.

NEWPORT HOUSE ⚑⚑

Kieran & Thelma Thompson
Newport
Co Mayo
Tel: (098) 41222
Fax: (098) 41613

There is something confidently, enjoyably patrician in the constitution of Kieran and Thelma Thompson's formidable house. Few others of the Irish country houses can match the elegant understatement of its luxury. We have described Newport House as a "well-tuned anachronism in the modern world", and such it is. This is the bourgeois dream at its most pertinent.

What fascinates, as much as the baleful calm of the house, is the thrilling kaleidoscope of clichés you fine here.

There are the ruddy-cheeked ghillies who wait around the hallway in the morning, anxious for fishing to begin. There is the impossibly stooped gardener, there are the engaging staff with their wise suggestions as to what you might enjoy for dinner, the ageing ladies who wait on the fringes of the dining room and who, should you stay long enough, will elide you under their wings and into their care.

Kieran Thompson describes the culinary philosophy of Newport as "allowing the quality of the food to come out". This is something John Gavan, the chef, a local man from Ballinrobe, manages with ease.

Richly creamy soups will follow the wonderful gravadlax. Turbot will enjoy a rich Champagne sauce, fresh salmon might be char-grilled and the voluble flavours cut by fresh vegetables from the walled garden behind the house.

After some salad leaves, a fine cheeseboard, and then a showypiece of desserts: crème caramel under an Ascot hat of spun sugar, home-made ice-cream in a flighty tuille basket. The wine list is splendid, and splendidly looked after by Cathal.

Some may find the dining room formal and hushed, filled as it will be with well-heeled Europeans, those record producers from Frankfurt, commercial lawyers, Frenchmen who went to the right école, all with elegant wives, best-behaviour kids.

Don't worry about this at all. "People say they feel they have been invited for a country weekend", says Mr Thompson, and you will, you will.

● **OPEN:** 7.30pm-9.30pm Mon-Sun. (Closed Oct-Mar).
● **ROOMS:** Eighteen rooms, all en suite.
● **AVERAGE PRICE:** B&B £50-£63 low season, £53-£66 high season per person sharing.
Single supplement £10.
Table d'hôte Dinner £29.
House Wine £10.
No Service Charge.
● **CREDIT CARDS:**
Visa, Access/Master, Amex, Diners.

● **NOTES:**
Full Licence.
Wheelchair Access (happy to help).
Children – high seats, cots, babysitting service, early evening dinner for kids.
The gates of Newport House are to be found just at the entrance to the village.

CROMLEACH LODGE ⓐⓡ
Christy & Moira Tighe
Ballindoon
nr Boyle
Co Sligo
Tel: (071) 65155
Fax: (071) 65455

Cromleach Lodge is a monument to painstaking application. Neither Christy nor Moira Tighe have a background in the business of running a restaurant with rooms, but their determination to improve, their will to succeed, has meant that Cromleach has steadily, steadily built an impressive reputation over the last years.

At the centre of this success is Moira Tighe's cooking, and her style exploits two central commands.

Firstly, she uses impeccable ingredients from local growers, the bulk of the vegetables and herbs being organically grown.

Secondly, thanks to being self-taught, and retaining the modesty which this gives a chef, her cooking strides confidently between transgressive improvisations – one of her best known dishes is a sausage of chicken mousse and crab, for example, served with a deliciously sweet carrot and Sauternes sauce – and a deep respect for the classic verities of the kitchen, which she is able to present as if newly invented.

These classics are perfectly achieved, thanks to sympathetic treatment and impeccable ingredients: beef fillet with a blue cheese sauce; stuffed quail with a pine nut glaze; a duet of salmon and turbot with a tomato compote; escalopes of veal on a grain mustard sauce. Timeless dishes and, here, vitalised by a creative kitchen.

Mrs Tighe admires the work of Anton Mosimann and other modern masters, and she loves bold colour and the intricate assembly of food on every plate.

This love of boldness is evident nowhere more so than with desserts, which are a speciality of Cromleach Lodge. Warm caramelised pineapple with an orange and honey glaze; barrels of local organic raspberries with a fruit coulis; a terrine of two chocolates with pistachio nuts. The sweet things in life, and how sweet to enjoy them here.

The rooms upstairs are excellent, and whilst they are imitative of standard hotel rooms, they balance this familiarity by being more thoughtful, more personalised, more welcoming, than one will find in any hotel. Service is excellent, breakfasts are terrific, and Cromleach has all the ingredients to prove to be an idyllic hideaway.

● **OPEN:** 7pm-9pm Mon-Sat, 6.30pm-8.30pm Sun. Closed Nov & Jan.
● **AVERAGE PRICE:** B&B £53-£65 per person sharing. Table d'hôte Dinner £30. House wine £12.95. No Service Charge.
● **CREDIT CARDS:**
Visa, Access/Master, Amex, Diners.

● **NOTES:**
Open over Xmas.
Restaurant Licence.
Wheelchair Access only with assistance.
Children – welcome.
Signposted from Castlebaldwin on the N4, 8 miles north west of Boyle.

GLEBE HOUSE ◐◐
Brid & Marc Torrades
Collooney
Co Sligo
Tel: (071) 67787

Brid Torrades has a skillfulness and an independence in her cooking which we might, perhaps, describe as Olneyesque.

Just as that great culinary master Richard Olney – one of the most celebrated and cultish figures in the world of food – is renowned for his ability to transform foods out of their original context, and to present them as if reborn, Mrs Torrades has the ability to take something simple – cabbage, for heaven's sake! – and, by virtue of shredding it and tossing it and dressing it with a little cream, you have a dish which is unbelievably pure, and gloriously unexpected. If this is cabbage, you say, then what is everyone else doing to it?

But Mrs Torrades can do this with all manner of food. And she does it subtly, quietly.

Glebe House is a modest, shoestring operation – they have found the money to improve the kitchen recently, and matters proceed gently, slowly – so there are no histrionics in the design, little that boasts of flamboyance.

Her imprimaturs in the kitchen – seasonality, self-sufficiency, clawing in as much local and, indeed, wild food as possible – guarantee food which is drenched with flavour.

She is happy to accept the description of a customer, who just happened to be a French chef, that her style of cooking is "Cuisine Bourgeois", and further defines her food as "very simple cooking. Simple and simply decorated, and you cook the food available at the time. Simplicity is the thing". Richard Olney might have said those very words.

This simplicity means that mussels in breadcrumbs with garlic butter will be perfect; fillet of beef with a green peppercorn sauce cooked appositely in the French way, which means it melts in the mouth; chicken with a basil cream sauce both voluptuous and energetic.

Some things may not work, but these are always the exception to a rule of successful, understated cooking. Salads and vegetables, from the garden, are bursting with flavour; sauces are spot on.

Summertime food in Glebe dances with fresh flavours, whilst autumn and winter cooking is consoling and comforting.

● **OPEN:** All year, dinner from 6.30pm-9.30pm Mon-Sun.
(Light lunches in summer from 1pm).
Shorter hours off season.
● **OPEN:** B&B £18.50-£25,
single room £24.
Table d'hôte Dinner £17.95.
House Wine £9.95. No Service Charge.
● **CREDIT CARDS:**
Visa, Access/Master, Amex, Diners.

● **NOTES:**
Wine Licence.
Wheelchair Access to restaurant only.
Children – high chairs, half price menu.
Signposted in Collooney, just before the railway bridge as you drive westwards out of the village, towards Sligo.

TEMPLE HOUSE ⚠ ✪
Sandy & Deb Perceval
Ballymote
Co Sligo
Tel: (071) 83329
Fax: (071) 83808

Few things in life are certain.

One of those few things, however, is the certainty, the absolute sureness you can feel when recommending to friends that they should take some time out and spend the couple of days, at their leisure, in Temple House.

"Brilliant place. Amazing food", says the luminary chef, delighted and consoled by Deb Perceval's delicious dinners.

"Brilliant place. The boys loved it", says the mother of those young monsters who, mysteriously, behaved like angels the whole time.

"Brilliant place. Great crack", say your parents, who went ceili dancing with other guests in the pubs up in the hills, after a dinner spent gabbing with all their new friends, and had the time of their life.

This is all you will ever hear about Temple House. It is a place of which no one ever speaks ill: a place about which you will only hear gushing, gushing praise, praise from the most diverse, irascible characters, the most unlikely sources.

And everyone, it seems, loves everything: in many country houses the idea of communal dining provokes a groan of anticipated boredom, but in Temple House everyone jabbers away amusingly the whole time, hungrily demolishing Deb's food, most of which has been grown, produced and reared by Sandy.

In other places, the eccentricities of the rooms might prove to be an inconvenience. Here, they are a fabulist distraction, a Gothic dream that weaves you into its weft.

The surreal, ancient waterworks are just one more vista of the Heath Robinson stratagem which keeps things working here, that slightly kooky, inimitable innocence which is everywhere. The company, of course, is always nice company, and you leave swapping cards, addresses, recipes, phone numbers, kisses, even.

Sandy and Deb Perceval control things at Temple House with Buddha-like patience and goodness, their sweetness and generosity never seeming to dip or dim.

● **OPEN:** Apr-Nov.
● **ROOMS:** Five rooms, four en suite, one with private bath.
● **AVERAGE PRICE:** B&B £40 per person sharing.
Set Dinner £17.
No Service Charge.
● **CREDIT CARDS:**
Visa, Access/Master, Amex, Diners.

● **NOTES:**
7.30pm dinner for guests only, book by 3pm.
Wine Licence.
No Wheelchair Access.
Children – welcome.
Temple House is 14 miles from Sligo and is signposted from the N17 Sligo to galway road. Travellers from Dublin should follow signs from the ESSO garage in Ballymote.

TRUFFLES ®✪
Bernadette O'Shea
The Mall
Sligo
Co Sligo
Tel: (071) 44226

"Pizza? What an odd, ordinary thing for one of America's most respected establishments to put on the menu, even in its relaxed café upstairs. When the pizza came and I tasted it, I saw what Alice Waters was about: the ordinary made extraordinary by the use of fine unusual ingredients... put together by a skillful and unusual taste".

This is the late, great Jane Grigson describing her first visit to the pizza café which the renowned American cook Alice Waters runs upstairs in her restaurant Chez Panisse, in San Francisco.

Mrs Grigson might have been writing for the thousands who have had a similar, equally epiphanous experience, in Bernadette O'Shea's restaurant, Truffles, in Sligo town.

"The ordinary made extra-ordinary". The ability to imagine and then enact an alchemical culinary brilliance is what sets Ms O'Shea apart. You don't eat her food and think: what a shame this lassie doesn't try something else and see how well she could do it, something serious.

Instead, you bite into the perfect alliance of light, essential dough and savour the startling succulence of the assembled ingredients and you realise, then, that you are eating food which is perfect.

How is it perfect? Because it is conceived and executed as a totality: this is pizza as total food: pizza as a template for organic tastes: pizza as a springboard for "fine unusual ingredients", pizza as an expression of great cooking skill and creativity.

And it must be stated that Ms O'Shea brooks no compromise when it comes to making pizza, least of all when it comes to her own commitment and involvement.

To watch her at work is to see a great artist moving confidently about her métier: the graceful rhythm, the intuitive grasp of colour and taste contrast; the split-second timing, the breathless delivery, the joy in her art.

You get great cooking in Truffles, and everything else to match: great fun, good wines, the coolest staff, the very best time. Jane Grigson would have loved it. Everybody else certainly does.

● **OPEN:** 5pm-10.30pm Tue-Sat.
● **AVERAGE PRICE:** À la carte Dinner £12.
House Wine £9.80.
No Service Charge.
● **CREDIT CARDS:** No Credit Cards.

● **NOTES:**
Wine Licence.
Wheelchair Access (but not to toilets or wine bar).
Children – welcome until 7pm.
Recommended for Vegetarians.
The Mall is an extension of Stephen's Street, on the main road from Sligo to Enniskillen, going towards Sligo General Hospital.

LEINSTER

the capital
city
and its

necklace
of

counties

KILGRANEY COUNTRY HOUSE ♠

Bryan Leech & Martin Marley
Bagenalstown, Co Carlow
Tel & Fax: (0503) 75283

The role of DNA in deciding whether people become hotel keepers or country house handlers has been little explored in scientific journals. It hasn't, come to think of it, even been explored on McNeil-Lehrer, or The Late Show. It hasn't even been debated on The Late Late Show, for heaven's sake.

But a Nobel Prize, or at least a six month contract in RTE, surely lies in wait for the person who can figure out the motivating impulse which inspires people to open their doors to the public.

We might conjecture, then, that Bryan Leech's decision to open Kilgraney Country House, a delightful, mellow house near Bagenalstown in County Carlow, surely owes something to the fact that his Mum, Mabel, was herself a celebrated B&B keeper for many years.

Whatever gifts Mrs Leech possesses, skills she continues to pass on through her involvement in the house, her son has inherited in full. He is, every inch, that character most beloved of hospitality guides: a charming host.

Kilgraney's prudish exterior and Presbyterian poise is cunningly offset by the furnishings which Bryan and Martin Marley have culled from their travels.

There are huge bright mirrors ringed in beaten stainless steel from the Philippines, modish chairs, in imitation of the female form, designed by Martin, artful concoctions made with coconut shell.

Kilgraney not only scores high in the World of Interiors stakes, however, for Mr Leech also wields a mean skillet: a perfectly achieved warm duck breast salad, an elderflower sorbet plosive with flavour, a droolsome array of fish and shellfish with a butter sauce, desserts such as chocolate truffle cake or an ice-cream bombe with a passion fruit sauce which are purest delight.

In the warm womb of the dining room, with its cheeky cherubs flittering around the cornice, as you sit and discuss Martin's amazing resemblance to Robert De Niro, it is hard to believe that the house is only an hour from Dublin, so perfect is its air of abandonment.

● **OPEN:** Weekends Mar-May, & Sept-Oct, weekly Jun-Aug.
● **ROOMS:** Five rooms, four en suite.
● **AVERAGE PRICE:**
£30-£35 per person sharing, £25 single.
Set dinner £22. House Wine £12.50.
No Service Charge.
● **CREDIT CARDS:**
Visa, Access/Master.

● **NOTES:**
Dinner, 8pm, for guests only, book by noon.
No Wheelchair Access.
Wine Licence.
Children – under 12 by arrangement only.
Just off the R705 (L18), 3.5miles (6km) from Bagenalstown (Muine Bheag) on the road heading towards Borris. Turn right at Kilgraney cross-roads and the house is the first entrance on the left.

AYUMI-YA JAPANESE RESTAURANT ⊗

Yoichi Hoashi
Newpark Centre
Newtownpark Ave, Blackrock
Tel: (01) 283 1767

AYUMI-YA JAPANESE STEAKHOUSE ⊗

132 Lower Baggot Street
Dublin 2
Tel: (01) 662 0233

There are many reasons why the Ayumi-Yas have prospered over the years – excellent cooking, a reverentially commodious atmosphere, steady adaptation to change, continual improvement – but the keynote of their success rests with the confidence and calmness of the service in both the Restaurant and the Steakhouse.

This has been a vital ingredient, for it has allowed Yoichi Hoashi to follow the brilliant example of his mother, Akiko, and to introduce the delicately delicious strictures of Japanese food to a public who might otherwise have been rather suspicious, rather quick to believe that Japanese cooking is austere and forbidding.

But, when you encounter the charming service of the Ayumis, service with grace and control, then the introduction to Japanese food becomes a gentle immersion into its delights.

The restaurants complement each other, the Blackrock space being more formal, with teppan-yaki tables and conventional and cushioned seating areas, whilst the basement of the Steakhouse and its noodle bar creates a more informal space. Together they offer a complete range of Japanese food, including the excellent Bento Box take-away service operated by the Steakhouse.

This may be the best take-away food in Dublin, and a God-send if you are self-catering.

But there is so much else to enjoy here: the fabulous, slurpsome noodles cooked in the Steakhouse – Soba, Udon, delicious Ramen – and the terrific range of dishes offered in the Restaurant – sublime tempura, great yakitori, magnificent vegetarian dishes, moreish shabu-shabu.

● **OPEN:** Steakhouse – 12.30pm-2.30pm Mon-Sat, 6pm-11.30pm Mon- Sat).
Restaurant – 6pm-11pm Mon-Sat, 5.30pm-9.45pm Sun.
● **AVERAGE PRICE:** Steakhouse Lunch and early evening menu from £6.95.
Dinner from £10.95.
Restaurant dinner from £15.50.
10% Service Charge in Restaurant.
10% Service Charge in Steakhouse after 6pm.
● **CREDIT CARDS:**
Visa, Access/Master, Amex, Diners.

● **NOTES:**
Children – welcome before 8.30pm in both restaurants.
Children's platters available, £6.50.
Wheelchair Access to Restaurant, but not to Steakhouse.
Both restaurants recommended for vegetarians, special menus available, £15.50.
Steakhouse is at the corner with Pembroke St. Restaurant is in a shopping centre on Newtownpark Road, south of the city.

CHESTNUT LODGE ⚠ ➔
**Nancy Malone
2 Vesey Place
Monkstown
Co Dublin
Tel: (01) 280 7860**

Nancy Malone's house is one of the finest places to stay in the city. Beautiful, high-ceilinged, the cream in the crop of a Georgian terrace, it is a svelte, consoling, uplifting place, and its location, in the quiet embrace of a quiet Monkstown road, near to the ferry at Dun Laoghaire, close to town but far enough away to give one a flavour of the villages of Dublin, merely adds to its splendour.

If its aspect is just right, it is further congratulated in the attention to small details which Nancy and her daughters ensure are correctly in place. Breakfast is a timeless joy: fine silver teapots and glistening cutlery, nutty soda bread and fresh orange juice at breakfast, delicious compotes and muesli which are one of Ms Malone's specialities – "Oh, when the strawberries are in season, my muesli is delicious!", she says, correctly – beautifully scrambled eggs with bacon, fine linen napery. The fact that such care is taken over every thing gives great pleasure, great reassurance. But making sure that everything is done properly is one of the things that Nancy does properly.

After a hard day's work in the big smoke, this is a lovely place to repair to for quiet, calmness. If you are just off the boat and beginning a holiday, then there is no better place to collect yourself and to begin to acquire those grace notes of the Irish holiday: hospitality, charm, true friendliness. "Nancy and her daughters were charming, and next time we will certainly stay there", writes a correspondent from England, just returned home and still dreaming of the delight of it all.

● **OPEN:** All year.
● **ROOMS:** Five rooms, four en suite.
● **AVERAGE PRICE:** B&B £27.50 per person sharing, £30-£35 single. No Service Charge.
● **CREDIT CARDS:** Visa, Access/Master

● **NOTES:**
Dinner on special request.
No Licence. No Wheelchair Access.
Children – welcome.
Recommended for Vegetarians.
No pets.
No car park.
Coming from Dublin direction, pass Monkstown Church, take the next turn right onto Sloperton Road.
Vesey Place is the terrace facing you.

CHINA-SICHUAN RESTAURANT ⚠
**David Hui
4 Lower Kilmacud Road,
Stillorgan, Co Dublin
Tel: (01) 288 4817
Fax: (01) 288 0882**

Banish from your mind the vague memory of those beloved sizzling dishes which you scoff, somewhat tipsy, on tipsy Saturday nights in your local Chinese eating house, those fake concoctions of MSG and culinary myopia.

Here, in David Hui's China-Sichuan, up in dreary, dull old Stillorgan, you will find the counterpoint to that hideously compromised cooking which we believe is Chinese food. In the China-Sichuan you find the real thing: Hot & Sour Soup with a musky, coffee-odoured thrill of a taste; pan fried dumplings with a fathom-black dipping sauce or in a hot sauce with spicy chilli; chicken in a garlic sauce, the dish offering endless nodes of viscous flavours; some monkfish with cashews perhaps, the fish jumping with freshness and the tentacular cuts putting you in mind of the roof of the Sydney Opera House.

With these, some voluptuously slinky Dan-Dan Mein noodles, or maybe some clean boiled rice. Mr Li, the cook, rarely puts a cleaver wrong, and the excitement of tastes which a dinner can deliver is one of the city's delights.

For dessert, then, some gloriously cool almond bean curd, the taste like an incredibly exotic marzipan, comes as a delicious surprise, the perfect ending to a series of surprisingly accessible and yet delightfully authentic tastes. Service is excellent, design is strictly unreconstructed over-the-top, and this is an invaluable Chinese restaurant.

● **OPEN:** 12.30pm-2.30pm,
6pm-11pm Mon-Sun.
(Lunch from 1pm Sun).
● **AVERAGE PRICE:** Lunch £8.
Dinner £16.50.
10% Service Charge.
● **CREDIT CARDS:**
Visa, Access/Master, Amex.

● **NOTES:**
Wine Licence.
Wheelchair Access to restaurant but not to toilet.
Children – welcome, high chairs.
Recommended for Vegetarians.
The restaurant is 100 yds from the Stillorgan Shopping Centre, on the Kilmacud Road, in the midst of a group of shops.

COOKE'S CAFÉ ⊛
John Cooke
14 South William Street, Dublin 2
Tel: (01) 679 0536/7/8

The changes visited on John Cooke's eponymous café over the last couple of years have been not just physical – the restaurant has expanded to provide for an "Upstairs" informal café and a "Downstairs" restaurant, and there is now a Food Hall in the building opposite – but also intellectual changes, which have seen the promise of this fine space blossom into real, creative, food.

Where, previously, the menus disported themselves amidst the complexities of Cal-Ital cooking and brought forth a range of dishes that were usually well-achieved but which seemed to present endless problems of service – it is extremely difficult to cook and sauce and serve pasta correctly, unless you are born in Bologna or are a spiritual heir of Marcella Hazan – the newer menus are much more compact and intelligent, and the troublesome pasta dishes are confined to a scattering of choices: fettucine al vodka, or angel hair with grilled aubergines, tomato, basil and olive oil as starters; angel hair vongole or tortelloni au gratin as main courses.

This has allowed more room for the strengths of the kitchen, both Upstairs and Downstairs. The seafood cookery is memorable – seabass en papillotte with a ragout of mussels, clams, saffron, tomato, herbs and olive oil is a knock-out compendium dish, whilst something as simple as fried calamari is perfectly executed. Experiments with offal and game are soulful: fine roast partridge with a celeriac purée; perfect duck liver with a concassé of tomato; veal liver and veal kidney both expertly cooked.

One gets the sense, also, that the kitchen is happier with this simpler, home-based style of food, so that air of frantic mishap which used to permeate the café is gone. Some things have not changed, however. Whilst the staff are slightly more relaxed than previously, they are still adolescently self-conscious. On a happier note, John Cooke's signature is still a byword for stylish, groovy food.

There are many other cooks in Dublin who are attempting something similar to Cooke's Café, but the original remains the best.

● **OPEN:** Restaurant – 12.30pm-3pm, 6pm-11pm.
"Upstairs" 10am-6pm (lunch from noon) Mon-Sun.
● **AVERAGE PRICE:** Table d'hôte Lunch £14.50, À la carte Dinner £30.
House wine £12.50. 10% Service Charge.
● **CREDIT CARDS:**
Visa, Access/Master, Amex, Diners.

● **NOTES:**
Wine Licence.
Wheelchair Access (with advance notice only).
Children – welcome.
At the back of the Powerscourt Townhouse Centre, on the corner at the zebra crossing.

LE COQ HARDI ®
John & Catherine Howard
35 Pembroke Road, Dublin 4
Tel: (01) 668 4130/668 9070

The public perception of John Howard's restaurant, throughout its long history, has always been of an archetypal bourgeois eating palace, somewhere that slings culinary history right back to the days of César Ritz and Auguste Escoffier, a restaurant which offers an un-interrupted blow-out of classic cuisine and claret.

Yet, whilst this image can be true, and whilst the restaurant does like to present itself as someplace where racehorse owners can land their helicopters after a successful day at the Curragh before they begin to fritter away their winnings on Haut-Brion and hâute cuisine – a tureen of Dublin Bay Prawns scented with cognac, a millefeuille of Irish salmon with a watercress butter sauce, a fricassée of monkfish with black noodles, coq au vin in a pastry dome – there is actually as much of the soft and ageless nature of French peasant cuisine to be found here as there is cooking that is grandiose and verbose.

You can enjoy long-cooked oxtail

braises, plump terrines of rabbit, chicken liver and leek, hake with tomato, olives, olive oil and mashed potato, Mr Howard's own invention of potato cakes with Clonakilty black pudding and fried apples. There will be perfectly cooked root vegetables, and the prices for the set meals are very fair.

If you do have a successful day at the Curragh, of course, then the carte in the Coq will soak up plenty of that easy-come money, and then there is one of the best and priciest wine lists in the entire country, just waiting to account for the rest.

- ● OPEN: Noon-2.30pm Mon-Fri, 7pm-11pm Mon-Sat.
- ● AVERAGE PRICE: Table d'hôte Lunch £18. Table d'hôte Dinner £30. 12.5% Service Charge.
- ● CREDIT CARDS: Visa, Access/Master, Amex, Diners.

- ● NOTES:
Full Restaurant Licence.
No Wheelchair Access.
Children – no facilities.
On the right hand side, when driving from Baggot Street towards the junction at Ballsbridge.

L'ECRIVAIN ◉ ✪
Derry & Sally Anne Clarke
112 Lwr Baggot Street, Dublin 2
Tel: (01) 661 1919, Fax: 661 0617

Derry Clarke's emergence as one of the most distinctive, creative cooks in Dublin has been achieved patiently and precisely, but it was the move to a less formal, more spacious room in 1995 which catal-

ysed the creativity of this kitchen, and since then L'Ecrivain has scarcely put a foot wrong.

It is a very friendly, very real operation, where spirited, professional people do their best to make sure you have a good time. There is no artifice to L'Ecrivain.

"Good food, good service, good value" is how Derry and Sally Anne Clarke describe their ambitions, but what is terrific about their restaurant is the fact that they achieve these objectives with such effect. They don't just talk about these ideals; they make sure they happen.

The main banker in Mr Clarke's cooking is a love of pure, generous flavours. It is typical of his style that he should make a Guinness sabayon for grilled oysters and rest them on a bed of spring cabbage. His prawns with a provençale sauce are flavourful to a point of sensory overload, john dory with a chilli sauce, or ravioli stuffed with duck rilette, are packed with melting flavour. Vegetarian dishes are especially inventive.

Derry Clarke's cooking now seems perfectly his own, truly Irish, truly at ease, his culinary signature nothing less than a high five of flavour. A word about the service: fantastic.

- ● OPEN: 12.30pm-2.30pm Mon-Fri, 6.30pm-11pm Mon-Sat.
- ● AVERAGE PRICE:
Table d'hôte Lunch £11.50-£14.50.
Table d'hôte Dinner £27.50.
House Wine £11.50.
10% Service Charge on food only.
- ● CREDIT CARDS:
Visa, Access/Master, Amex, Diners.

● NOTES:
Full Licence.
No Wheelchair Access.
Children – no facilities.
Recommended for Vegetarians.
In a courtyard, beside Lad Lane, on Baggot
Street, opposite the Bank of Ireland.

ELEPHANT & CASTLE ®
Liz Mee & John Hayes
18 Temple Bar
Dublin 2
Tel: (01) 679 3121

Ever since it opened, in the late 1980s, many people seem to have imagined that the success of the Elephant & Castle from the day it opened its doors was, and is, based on some simple formula, something you merely have to crack into and, voila!, you too will be in charge of a restaurant which is packed to the rafters morning, noon and night.

The truth of the matter, of course, is that no one has succeeded in replicating the success of this potent palace of food.

The failure of the copy-cats has lain, usually, in their refusal to believe that there is, in fact, no formula behind this simple, bare-floorboards 'n' t-shirts place. If there is no formula, however, then perhaps there is a secret, and we might borrow an album title from R.E.M., those aristocrats of rock'n'roll, and say that the secret of the E&C, the secret of its Monster success, is that it is Automatic For The People.

Night and day, it serves the food you want, and becomes the place you want it to be. From 8-in-the-morning omelette breakfasts, to a mid-morning gouter, to a pasta lunch with a girlfriend, maybe a late afternoon pick-me-up tuna and guacamole sandwich, or pre-theatre chicken wings that have you licking your fingers right through the performance, then onwards to a late night romantic rendezvous with a loved-one, even post-pub burger and fried potatoes, perhaps a family table for Sunday brunch.

All of the foods for all of these occasions can be found here.

The food is democratically priced, but never cheap: with these ingredients it could never be. The basic menu has evolved little, and any innovation and experimentation comes from the daily specials: lamb korma with relishes; fettucini with chicken, shiitake mushrooms and asparagus, grilled fillet steak and rouille served with herb mashed potato; Sichuan chicken with spicy stir-fried noodles. Whatever you eat, it will be part of an ideal of service and simplicity which announces itself as Automatic For The People.

● OPEN: 8am-11.30pm Mon-Fri,
10.30am-midnight Sat, noon-11.30pm Sun.
● AVERAGE PRICE:
Lunch £3-£7. Dinner £15.
No Service Charge (except for groups of 8 or more, 10%).
● CREDIT CARDS:
Visa, Access/Master, Amex, Diners.

● NOTES:
Wine Licence.
Wheelchair Access.
Children – welcome.
In Dublin's Temple Bar, just on the south side of the River Liffey.

GIROLLES ⊛

Gary & Helen Morris
64 Sth William Street
Dublin 2
Tel: (01) 679 7699

Gary Morris' cooking wears big, ruddy flavours proudly, and he has quickly forged his own style in the little space that is Girolles, with everything centred around duets and duos: man and wife, food and wine; cooking which is playfully engaged with itself.

So, with a stuffed saddle of rabbit he will serve a little rilette of rabbit, while with pheasant he will add a tiny game pie. He will grill goat's cheese and echo the effect by adding both a herb crust and a crouton. Everything Gary Morris cooks looks to find an echo of the principal ingredient, and this makes his food not only clever, but very well conceived and involving.

But it isn't smartypants cooking, not by any means. Mr Morris loves rustic flavours too much to lose sight of the fact that his strength lies with coaxing unadulterated goodness out of his chosen ingredients: braised beef with wild mushrooms and a celeriac mash: wild duck and venison pie with an onion marmalade; mussel broth with saffron and barley; Wicklow lamb with white haricot beans, smoked bacon and colcannon.

This food calls for an appetite, and then satisfies that appetite with delight. It is friendly, unpretentious food in a friendly, unpretentious place.

- **OPEN:** 12.30pm-2.15pm Tue-Fri, 6pm-11pm Tue-Sat, 5pm-10pm Sun.
- **AVERAGE PRICE:** Table d'hôte Lunch £12.50. Table d'hôte Dinner £18. No Service Charge. House Wine £9.95.
- **CREDIT CARDS:** Visa, Access/Master, Amex, Diners.
- **NOTES:** Wine Licence. Children – welcome. No Wheelchair Access. Near the corner with Wicklow Street.

RESTAURANT PATRICK GUILBAUD ⊛

Patrick Guilbaud
46 James Place
Baggot Street Lwr, Dublin 2
Tel: (01) 676 4192

Patrick Guilbaud's eponymous restaurant is claustral in its pursuit of a classic idea of French food, as pernickety as Martin Luther when it comes to the edicts of cooking. "We are very classical", M. Guilbaud will tell you. "All our sauces are the way they should be done. If we say we do a beurre blanc we do a beurre blanc, if we do a bearnaise we do a bearnaise, but the real way. We do everything the way it should be done".

And this is true, and can make, on occasion, for exceptional eating in an elegant space: lobster ravioli on savoy cabbage; turbot with a Seville orange and ginger sauce; roast monkfish basted with honey and balsamic vinegar; veal sweetbreads with lemon and coriander; pig's trotters with a wild mushroom pudding.

The precision of tastes which chef Guillaume Lebrun can disclose from ingredients is never less than impressive, though curiously, the seasoning of the dishes is always slightly persistent and aggressive.

And yet, despite the protestations of affection and delight from many who have eaten here over the past dozen years, for many more Guilbaud's is a restaurant that is easy to admire, yet difficult to love.

Of course you admire the hard-headed determination, the well-drilled staff with their cloche synchronicity honed to the nth degree, the keenness of the prices for set menus, and what Molly O'Neill of the New York Times called "the refined restraint of his cuisine".

And one must always bear in mind that Patrick Guilbaud opened his restaurant at a time when the climate of Dublin culinary opinion cared little for creative, accomplished cooking and a devout professionalism in the business of running a restaurant. He succeeded, in many ways, against the odds.

But admiring is one thing, and affection another, and Guilbaud's has never dispensed with its air of cool distance, of knowingness. This makes it perfect for entertaining, of course, for they get on with their work while you get on with yours and they never, but never, get in the way.

But, if you cherish humour, spontaneity, and cooking that comes from the heart as well as the head, then other cooks, and other restaurants in the city, may prove more beguiling.

● **OPEN:** 12.30pm-2pm, 7.30pm-10.15pm Tues-Sat.
● **AVERAGE PRICE:**
Table d'hôte Lunch £18.50,
Table d'hôte Dinner from £30.
15% Service Charge.
● **CREDIT CARDS:**
Visa, Access/Master, Amex, Diners.

● **NOTES:**
Full Licence.
Wheelchair Access. Children – high chair.
In a lane behind the Bank of Ireland, on Baggot Street.

NUMBER 31 ◎⊝
Brian & Mary Bennett
31 Leeson Close, Dublin 2
Tel: (01) 676 5011
Fax: (01) 676 2929

Number 31 is now such an essential, indispensable part of the city that you wonder how you survived before its collusion of avant garde architecture and old fashioned hospitality arrived.

The location of Brian and Mary Bennett's house, in a quiet mews just off the strip of Leeson Street, means that the entire city is within walking distance. This means that visitors feel they are truly in the city, for Dublin makes more sense when seen on foot, for then one appreciates the scale of this small precise metropolis.

The reputation of Number 31 has spread at the pace of a bush fire, with the same people coming back, followed quickly by the droves of friends to whom they have recommended – insisted – that this is where you stay when in Dublin.

One of the pleasures of the house is the sense of surprise it engenders: the secret centre of lean design and minimalist restraint which lies behind those high stone walls and that big wooden door. Like a Faberge egg, the house unfurls hidden elements to you at each turn, in the sunken recess of the sitting room, in the bright capaciousness of the breakfast room.

One will hear praise for the breakfasts from starred chefs; praise for the style of the house from much-travelled writers; praise galore from holidaymakers who discover this little miracle of modernist design. The extension of the house, to assume the elegant, spacious mantle of the principal house on Fitzwilliam Place to which Number 31 was the original mews, is a new birth for a splendid venture which makes it bigger, better, and more essential to the city of Dublin.

● **OPEN:** All year
● **ROOMS:** Eighteen rooms, all en suite, one with sauna
● **AVERAGE PRICE:** B&B from £34 per person sharing, £40 single.
No Extra Charges
● **CREDIT CARDS:**
Visa, Access/Master

● **NOTES:**
No Restaurant facilities.
No Licence.
Wheelchair Access (possible with assistance, room on ground floor).
Children – over 12 only.
No pets.
Secure car park.
Leeson Close runs off Lower Leeson Street (opposite 42 Lower Leeson Street).

101 TALBOT ☺
Margaret Duffy & Pascal Bradley
101-102 Talbot Street
Dublin 1
Tel: (01) 874 5011

Margaret Duffy and Pascal Bradley's 101 Talbot has quietly manoeuvred itself into a position where it is not just one of the best restaurants in the capital, and not just one of the most admired, but easily one of the most enjoyed, and enjoyable.

Everything this astute and amusing pair do is devoted to making 101 a special space in which to enjoy good food, good wine, good times. Walk up the stairs, away from the interesting grot of Talbot Street, and this cocoon of calm space, cool sounds, funky grub and sweet service sets your soul at ease. That is the kind of place it is: the restaurant that is home from home.

You can cast your mind back over many meals eaten here during the last few years – lunches with mile-a-minute gossip amongst your mates, quiet solo mid-afternoons with just some pasta and the newspaper to peruse, happy dinners where bottle after bottle of Fetzer Fumé Blanc or Wolfie Blass's Cab Sauv are resolutely demolished in the cause of good cheer – and what is consistent is just how much the charm, the youthfulness and the bonhomie of 101 has contributed to the cause of enjoying lunch or dinner.

Margaret Duffy's food always tastes like something which she has, firstly, enjoyed cooking and, second-ly, something which she would like to eat herself.

The food is so enjoyably friendly, so

goddamned consumable!, for good-ness sake, that you will likely find yourself day-dreaming about that parsnip soup, or that perfectly baked fillet of cod, you will find yourself fondly recalling that brioche of vegetables with a blue cheese dressing, or that clever dish where chicken is stuffed with olives, sun-dried tomatoes and mozzarella, years later you will recall the excellence of that pecan pie or those oranges in caramel and Cointreau.

The personality of 101 is exuded through the food and the great service, and this bubbly, warm personality is what makes 101 so special. Without Margaret and Pascal, the chances are that it would be just another restaurant space. Thanks to them, and their lack of pretension, their wisdom, it is completely invaluable.

● **OPEN:** 10am-3pm Mon,
10am-11pm Tue-Sat.
Lunch served noon-3pm.
Dinner served 6pm-11pm.
● **AVERAGE PRICE:**
Lunch £3.50-£10.
Dinner £12-£15.
Minimum charge £3.50 during peak times.
No Service Charge.
(except for groups of 8 or more, 10%).
● **CREDIT CARDS:**
Visa, Access/Master, Amex, Diners.

● **NOTES:**
Full Bar Licence.
No Wheelchair Access.
Children – welcome, high chairs.
Recommended for Vegetarians.
Talbot Street runs parallel to Abbey Street, and 101 about one hundred yards down from O'Connell Street.

CONRAD GALLAGHER'S PEACOCK ALLEY ®✪
Conrad Gallagher
47 South William Street, Dublin 2
Tel: (01) 662 0760/662 0776

The good news about Conrad Gallagher's move to his bright, summery new home on South William Street, is that a lot more people will be able to enjoy his food. And enjoying his food is what this young man's work is all about. In tandem with a handful of other chefs, he has revolutionised the restaurant scene in the capital, suddenly firing off salvos and standards which are frantically catching up with the best of Belfast and Cork. But, whatever they may do up north and in the deep south, there is no one else in the country with a style like Mr Gallagher.

He is not just a great cook, he is a great dreamer. Some of his food is so outrageously created, confected and sculptured that it seems impossible to believe it could be born of the same simple ingredients which every other chef uses.

He is the Gaudi of Dublin cooks, his work spiralling into an unbelievable ascent to the heavens, an involved, arch, architectural inventing of food.

Conrad Gallagher describes his style as "Mediterranean Provincial Cooking", and this gives a clue to his intentions, for he loves extracting the inherent sweetness of foods, he loves unveiling the sunshine.

A dish such as ravioli with lobster, tomato and goat cheese is a perfect illustration of his strengths, and dinner sees this chef finding alliances and sympathies in everything he cooks: chicken stuffed with organic greens with a red pepper polenta; turbot with a broth of black and white beans; rack of lamb with rosemary mashed potatoes; gratin of oyster with a blanket of leeks and a shallot and tarragon custard.

It is gorgeous food, and in these adroitly fashionable rooms, with their splendidly youthful and funky staff, it makes for something unforgettable.

Peacock Alley offers food that is nothing less than thrilling, for it offers a chance to share the intoxicating, transfixing pleasure of the work of a chef at full tilt, at full speed, at full throttle.

Conrad Gallagher holds nothing back. There are no compromises, no shortcuts, no concessions, and you should simply abandon yourself to the sensual thrill of food which boasts and profits from a devilish creativity and a raucous excitement.

● **OPEN:** 12.30pm-2.30pm, 6.30pm-11pm Mon-Sat.
● **AVERAGE PRICE:**
Table d'hôte Lunch £15.95.
À la carte Dinner £27.
10% Service Charge. House Wine £12.
● **CREDIT CARDS:**
Visa, Access/Master, Amex, Diners.

● **NOTES:**
Full licence.
Children – no facilities.
Recommended for vegetarians.
South William Street runs parallel to Grafton Street. Peacock Alley is about half way up, on the left hand side, as you drive the one-way street.

RED BANK RESTAURANT ◎
Terry McCoy
7 Church Street, Skerries,
Co Dublin
Tel: (01) 849 1005
Fax: (01) 849 1598

The way Terry McCoy does it, being chef and patron of a restaurant seems a piece of cake.

First, source your foods from local growers, local suppliers, local fishmongers and fish smokers.

Get your oysters from Carlingford Lough, conveniently just up the road. Get your flour from local flour grinders, in this case The White River Mill, in Dunleer, conveniently just up the road. You do this in order that the foods of the region will have the tastes of the region.

What you do, then, is to complete the equation, and cook them in the region, exploiting your own techniques, and gently introduce the occasional innovation that has come from a trip abroad, where you learnt of some alliance or some suitable technique, which you find can be made to work in your own kitchen.

Cook, then, with grace and good humour, and get things right: steamed cockles and oysters; hake with the energetic kick of horseradish; warm smoked salmon with a tarragon cream; crab meat mixed with sherry and cream before baking; haddock – and here we see the influence of travel – with Creole spices; wings of skate with spring onions, perhaps a smoked loin of pork, or roasted Barbary duck.

The meat dishes in The Red Bank, like everything else, will be correct and flavourful, but it is with fish and shellfish that Mr McCoy shines, and you find yourself going "ooh" and "aah" with pleasure at the succulence and promise of each mouthful.

McCoy's object, as he himself will say, is to treat the foods with "sympathy and respect". But he also knows that fish cookery is all about sources – local sources – and sauces. And he knows this better than just about anyone. Expect to have a great time.

- **OPEN:** 7pm-10pm Tue-Sat, 12.30pm-2.15pm Sun.
- **AVERAGE PRICE:**
Sunday Lunch £13.75.
Table d'hôte Dinner £20.
No Service Charge.
- **CREDIT CARDS:**
Visa, Access/Master, Amex, Diners.

- **NOTES:**
Restaurant Licence.
Wheelchair Access.
Children – controlled children welcome
Skerries is 29km north of Dublin and signposted from the N1 Dublin/Belfast road. The restaurant is in the town centre.

ROLY'S BISTRO ®
Roly Saul, Colin O'Daly
7 Ballsbridge Terrace
Dublin 4
Tel: (01) 668 2611

Roly Saul's eponymous restaurant is the greatest success story in Ireland's restaurant culture in recent years, and its success is richly deserved.

Indeed, if there is a reward on this earth for initiative, innovation, creativity and professionalism, Mr Saul and his team deserve it more than most.

Their secret has lain with the assembly of the dream team who run the place: John O'Sullivan who handles the paperwork; Roly Saul who masterminds meeting and greeting and the extraordinary business of seating people, a task so complicated he refers to it as "3-D chess".

And the lynch-pin of the team is Colin O'Daly, a chef who has metamorphosed from an intricate, involved cook into a Bistro Barnstormer without the slightest sign of tension.

Mr O'Daly's contribution is to create, demand and insist upon food of a superbly high standard, to insist on correctness of preparation and presentation. For what you get in Roly's – aside from a restaurant space of exquisite elegance and comfort, aside from staff who are dedicated and mindblowingly efficient – is food which is much, much better than you have a right to expect, given the price they charge. Roly's is the best bargain in Irish food, because you get the finest food at the finest price.

And they do not cut corners. There are no shortcuts, no edges trimmed. The food – roasted leg of lamb, game pie with cranberries, chicken niçoise, salmon trout with a fennel and saffron sauce, a smoked fish cake, and a crêpe stuffed with spinach, oyster mushrooms, Swiss cheese and sesame seeds as the vegetarian choice – are typical of the array of main courses offered on a week's menu.

All of them will be correctly cooked, and bright and voluptuous with flavour, dishes which fuse slap-happy bistro flavours with a refinement worthy of a brasserie.

Best of all, Roly's is a fun place. No matter whether you are eight or eighty, the secret of Roly's success is that you can extract from it what you want: a quick lunch or a lingering dinner, a family party, a night out with the girls – Roly's has an enormous proportion of female customers, interestingly – dinner a deux. The wine list is wonderful and terrific value. But then, you suspected as much, didn't you?

● **OPEN:**
Noon-2.45pm, 6pm-10pm Mon-Sun.
● **AVERAGE PRICE:**
Table d'hôte Lunch £9.50.
Table d'hôte Dinner from £15.
10% Service Charge.
● **CREDIT CARDS:**
Visa, Access/Master, Amex, Diners

● **NOTES:**
Restaurant Licence.
Wheelchair Access.
Children – no special facilities.
On the corner between Ballsbridge and Herbert Park, just down from the American Embassy.

SAAGAR ◎
Sunil & Meera Kumar
16 Harcourt Street
Dublin 2
Tel: (01) 475 5060

Sunil and Meera Kumar have run the celebrated Indian restaurant, Little India, in Mullingar since 1992,

and the Saagar has benefited enormously from their experience.

It is a sleek, pristine operation, housed in a basement on Harcourt Street, and the attention to detail is dazzling: crisp blue-white linen, gleaming glasses, sparkling cutlery, and the deft assurance of Nisheeth Tak, the manager, quickly swaddle you in the restaurant's cheery charm.

The menu is extensive – more than a dozen starters, a multiplicity of main courses, numerous bread and rice creations – and it aims to explore the regional cooking of India, as well as offering novel creations of the chefs, such as murgh dumpukht, a mild chicken dish with a coconut and almond base which is sweet, nutty and delicious.

Actually choosing what you want to eat is agonising, but confident expertise, then, is the hallmark of the kitchen: excellent tandoori chicken is succulent and tender, just right: a fine, spicy hot Colombo fish curry with southern Indian seasoning sends the mouth delectably into orbit.

The wine list is good, and whilst some may find the presence of fine wines on the list of an Indian restaurant rather strange, the temperateness of most of the dishes in the Saagar makes them suitable partners for a good bottle.

"I got the impression that the wine, like ourselves, was in good hands" said a friend. Prices, for such fine service and food, are enjoyably modest.

● **OPEN:** 12.30pm-3pm Mon-Fri, 6pm-11.30pm Mon-Sun.

● **AVERAGE PRICE:**
À La carte Lunch under £10.
Table d'hôte Dinner over £16.
No Service Charge.
● **CREDIT CARDS:**
Visa, Access/Master, Amex, Diners.
● **NOTES:**
Children – welcome.
Wine Licence. No Wheelchair Access.
Harcourt Street runs off St Stephen's
Green.

LA STAMPA ⊛
Paul Flynn
35 Dawson Street, Dublin 2
Tel: (01) 677 8611/677 3336

Paul Flynn is such a fine cook that
one wishes he had a benefactor who
would grant him a small restaurant,
a large kitchen brigade, and a
beautiful room in which to serve his
creations.

Well, he has the last of this trilogy
of dreams – La Stampa, a converted
guildhall, is the most glorious
restaurant room in the city.

But, in the real world of commerce
in which restaurants must work, Mr
Flynn cooks in a restaurant which
turns over very large numbers of
covers. And he manages it with a
small brigade.

And Mr Flynn is such a good cook
that, despite the pressures of this
system, he still creates good food.
We must ascribe this, perhaps, to the
discipline learnt at the right hand of
the tempestuous Nico Ladenis, with
whom Mr Flynn worked in his
various London restaurants for
almost a decade. The discipline of
fine fish cookery which he learnt
there still stands to him: baked sea

bream with a dash of sesame oil is
one of those successes whose merit
rests entirely on simplicity and
timing, and confidence.

It is the sort of dish, also, with
which Mr Flynn seems most at
home. He appears to have abandoned the early, modish revisions of
certain Irish staples like colcannon,
or bacon and cabbage, which used
to feature, and he is most at home
with classic bistro fare such as confit
of duck, or – again a dish which
needs simplicity, timing and confidence – pan fried calf's liver, or the
calf's liver grilled with pancetta.
These are his dishes, and they are the
dishes to go for: he is a purist, not an
innovator, and most at home with
brasserie standbys such as boudin of
chicken, or millefeuille of lamb, or a
blanquette of veal.

Any description of La stampa
must mention the restaurant manager, Declan Maxwell. Mr Maxwell
is a genius at people-handling, and it
is purest joy just to watch him at
work.

● **OPEN:** 12.30pm-2.30pm Mon-Fri,
6.30pm-11.15pm Mon-Sun,
('till 11.45pm Fri & Sat).
● **AVERAGE PRICE:** Table d'hôte Lunch
£10.50, À la carte Dinner from £20.
No Service Charte (except for parties of 6
or more, 10%).
● **CREDIT CARDS:**
Visa, Access/Master, Amex, Diners.

● **NOTES:**
Restaurant Licence.
No Wheelchair Access.
Children – no facilities.
Opposite the Mansion House at the St.
Stephen's Green end of Dawson Street.

THORNTON'S ⓡ⭐
Kevin Thornton
1 Portobello Road
Dublin 8
Tel: (01) 454 9067

Kevin Thornton is the Renaissance man of the professional kitchen. His work demonstrates such a capacious fluidity, such a profound inventiveness, such total intellectual command, that no one else in the capital can rival him for originality.

He can do anything, and Dublin is fortunate that this great chef, with his great skills, is a man who devotes his talent to his work, and has no time for egotism or immature showing off.

He approaches his work as a vocation, and finds in it a complete intellectual and artistic satisfaction, which means that one envies him the pleasures which cooking gives him, but one remains thankful that you are the customer who will reap the benefits of his devotion.

This sense of a vocation means that Mr Thornton can achieve a style which is engagingly abstract, with ingredients utilised in truly novel ways, but he never loses sight of the simple truth: "Food is about flavour", he says, simple as that.

And what flavours! This is cooking with an unrestrained richness, a voluptuousness. It has become fashionable to deprecate this aspect of cooking, and to preach the minimalist ethic as being not only good for our hearts but also – in some curious way – as good for our souls. Well, maybe ascetics would not enjoy the richness of a fillet of turbot with pommes purée and the adroit accompaniment of a grapefruit and beetroot sauce, but aesthetes will love the luxurious style of the dish, its fulsomeness balanced by sweet batons of beet and tart curves of grapefruit.

They will, likewise, love the intensity in a starter such as a tomato and basil tartlet with pesto, served with a red pepper oil. Little coins of green pepper and tomato are arranged around the top of the tart, from which a crisp fried basil leaf ascends like a Brancusi sculpture. It is handsome, and handsomely intense in flavour, the red pepper oil a foil for the sweet pesto. Indeed, the use of flavoured oils and vinaigrettes has become a signature of Kevin Thornton's cooking, with the menu offering truffle and balsamic vinaigrettes, gazpacho and light garlic sauces, and the red pepper may appear again, alongside squid ink, as a sauce to accompany fillet of red mullet.

The restaurant is elegantly simple, the service sublime, the music fabulous, and the passion and the artistry evident here is Beethovinian.

● **OPEN:** 7pm-10.30pm Tue-Sat.
● **AVERAGE PRICE:**
Table d'hôte Dinner from £28.
10% Service Charge.
● **CREDIT CARDS:**
Visa, Access/Master, Amex, Diners.

● **NOTES:**
Wine Licence.
No Wheelchair Access.
Children – no facilities.
On the Grand Canal between the Rathmines and Harold's Cross bridges.

TONLEGEE HOUSE ⓇⒶ

Mark & Marjorie Molloy
Athy
Co Kildare
Tel & Fax: (0507) 31473

Here is a good dinner table game to play, especially if you are out on a first date with someone, and you have brought them to dinner at Tonlegee House.

Put your heads together, and think of the great boy-girl double acts in history.

Think of Antony and Cleo. Fred and Ginger. Bonny and Clyde. Comden and Green.

Yes, okay then, your Mum and Dad. If you must.

Discuss all this in the darkened womb of a room which is the dining room at Tonlegee.

Chat away as dinner begins. Start with the millefeuille of crab meat with a grain mustard sauce, a beautifully involved creation of Mark Molloy's, ribboned with strips of vegetables and fresh as the sea itself.

Okay, then, Richard and Judy.

Move along with a cracking bowl of cream of celery and blue cheese, into which you spoonishly dip the super breads.

Peters and Lee? Come on!

Marjorie Molloy, as you ponder all this, will be getting on with things all around and about you, to the manner born.

Then a breast of guinea fowl, served with a ballotine of its leg, the roast garlic and thyme precise and suitable bedfellows for the rich flesh. Perfect purée of potatoes, crisp

leaves of spinach. A beautiful dish.

Fanny and Johnnie, she remembers. The late Fanny and Johnnie.

Fanny and Johnnie! You must be joking!

Out of the choice of desserts, you opt for a crisp, just-right lemon tart with some vanilla ice cream.

It has been a perfect dinner.

Depending on just how you are getting on at this point, how confident you are feeling, how much wine you have drunk, you might say: You and Me?

Don't know about that, says your date.

But, you say, if there is a better double act in the restaurant business than Mark and Marjorie Molloy, if there is a couple so respectively good at their job both front and back of house, then I don't know who they are.

Neither do we. Mark and Marjorie. The dream team.

● **OPEN:** All year.
Dinner served 7pm-9.30pm Mon-Thur,
7pm-10.30pm Fri-Sat.
● **ROOMS:** Nine rooms, all en suite.
● **AVERAGE PRICE:**
B&B £30 per person sharing.
Dinner £20-£22. No Service Charge.
● **CREDIT CARDS:** Visa, Access/Master.

● **NOTES:**
Sun night dinner for residents only.
Full Licence.
No Wheelchair Access
(though happy to help).
Children – welcome, cot, high chair.
In Athy, cross two bridges and take the Kilkenny road out of town. Very soon you will see their sign telling you to go left.

Amazing food & Beds ensuite

LACKEN HOUSE ⊗⊗ ✪
Eugene & Breda McSweeney
Dublin Road
Kilkenny
Co Kilkenny
Tel: (056) 61085
Fax: (056) 62435

Invention and tradition.

Regionalism and internationalism. The personal and the professional. That diplomat of good food, Eugene McSweeney, brings all these ingredients together in his cooking in Lacken House, fuses these competing pressures perfectly into a cuisine which is proud and proudly delicious.

You could select any dish from the menus which Mr McSweeney prepares and cooks in Lacken House, a homely, peaceful restaurant with rooms which he and his wife Breda run just on the outskirts of Kilkenny, and no matter what the choice, and no matter what the individual tastes and the distinct techniques which will be involved, you will find yourself always confronted by two simple truths.

The first is that with everything he cooks, Mr McSweeney exploits the long-learnt skill of the professional cook. Skill, here, is used to extract flavour, to reveal the character and essence of a food. Starters such as a warm salad with Dunmore East scallops, or a tartlet of lambs' kidneys in a light mustard sauce, or black pudding on boxty with a sage butter sauce, will taste as good as they can possibly taste. They will taste, quite simply, of themselves.

Secondly, you will also find that the cooking shows someone who has never lost touch with the scents, attractions and satisfactions of the garden and the ground: a splendid nettle pesto served with a simple vegetable soup; breast of chicken on roasted beetroot; loin of lamb with a tansy mousse. These green, wild tasting of herbs and leaves offer a counterpoint to the luxury of fillet of beef or crispy duckling.

A wise cook, Mr McSweeney keeps his chain of suppliers as short as possible, though he will wander down as far south as Clonakilty to secure Edward Twomey's black pudding in order to make his lively twice-baked black pudding soufflé. Otherwise, everything is local.

And local, also, is the character of Lacken House, the staff are warmly welcoming, and you find the true tastes of Irish food, and Irish hospitality, here. Breda McSweeney is one of the finest sommeliers in the country, and her expertise is the perfect addendum to her husband's inventiveness and perfectionism.

● **OPEN:** All year.
Dinner 7pm-10.30pm Tue-Sat.
● **ROOMS:** Eight bedrooms, all en suite.
● **AVERAGE PRICE:** B&B £30.
Dinner £23. No Service Charge.
● **CREDIT CARDS:**
Visa, Access/Master, Amex, Diners.

● **NOTES:**
Restaurant Licence. No Wheelchair Access.
Children – high chair and special menu.
Recommended for Vegetarians.
On the Dublin Road just as you drive into Kilkenny from the north, just past the roundabout.

THE MOTTE ®
**Alan Walton &
Tom Reade-Duncan
Inistioge
Co Kilkenny
Tel: (056) 58655**

There is a great sense of playfulness and enjoyment about the food, the cooking and the atmosphere in The Motte, and they really do like to have fun with their cooking, do Alan and Tom.

Smoked duck breast with raspberry lentils, or maybe that duck breast with a black bean sauce.

Calves liver with grilled pineapple.

Gorgonzola burger.

A bacon, prawn and lettuce tartlet.

Duck liver mousse with cumberland sauce.

Slightly strange combinations, slightly unexpected, but well achieved, carefully considered, when you come to consider it. And fun. Yes, fun.

They have always enjoyed this playfulness with ingredients, even back when the Motte was situated in the centre of Inistioge, before it moved to its brand new home just a few hundred yards outside the most filmed and photographed village in the country.

In the early days, when the restaurant was back in the village, when you might be served pork fillet cooked in coconut milk, or roast pheasant with a chocolate sauce, they were busy having fun with food, adding twists and turns that caused you to light up with pleasure.

Clever, fun food, and very well controlled.

But, of course, they are prudent restaurateurs, not just showmen, and so alongside their inventions and improvisations, there is a rock solid selection of ever-popular dishes.

Swordfish steak with a red wine, mint and olive sauce.

Venison steak with a beetroot and orange glaze.

Rabbit terrine with tomato chutney.

Stuffed guinea fowl with a sherry and redcurrant sauce.

Barbary duck with a wild mushroom and pine nut sauce.

But, even if you shy clear of the more outlandish and inventive dishes on the menu and play it somewhat safe, the central rule of The Motte is ever-present: this is a fun place, somewhere to have a good time. Alan and Tom work hard to make sure that happens.

● **OPEN:** 7pm-9.30pm Wed-Sun
(open Tue Jun-Sept).
● **AVERAGE PRICE:**
Table d'hôte Dinner £18.90.
No Service Charge.
● **CREDIT CARDS:**
Visa, Access/Master, Amex.

● **NOTES:**
Wine Licence.
Wheelchair Access, but not to toilets.
Children – no facilities.
Vegetarian dinner with 24 hours prior notice.
The Motte is 500 yards from Inistioge, heading over the bridge as you drive towards Kilkenny.

CHEZ NOUS ⚆
Audrey Canavan
Kilminchy
Portlaoise, Co Laois
Tel: (0502) 21251

"A lovely, warm-hearted person" is the kind of thing people will tell you about Audrey Canavan, and you will hear no word of argument from anyone who has ever stayed at her cute bungalow, just adjacent to the main N7 Dublin-Cork road.

Mrs Canavan's ability to make a stop-over into an event is legendary. You might find yourself at Chez Nous, the first time, just because it is so convenient to the main road, just because you can't face driving all the way to Cork or to Dublin, because it is late and you are tired or don't know the road, or whatever.

But the second time you stay at Chez Nous will be because you want to stay there, because you want to indulge in the plenitude of Audrey's personality, and her fine food.

Breakfast is ordered at night, and may, unexpectedly, cause some sleepless anxiety.

If, for example, you choose the "Clonakilty Black Pudding cooked in Duck Fat with grated Apple and Carrot", this will mean that you are passing over the "Potato Cakes with Lashings of Pure Irish Butter and Sea salt".

And how can you resist a dish which so sumptuously promises "Lashings" of butter? If only you had two stomachs. Nothing for it but to stay another day.

A correspondent described Audrey's breakfast table as "the most opulent looking table which we have ever seen in a B&B – flowers, home-made jams and marmalades, home-made bread, home-made scones, home-made biscuits, toast, tea, coffee... All this against the background of the garden and bathed in the soft light of an early Autumn morning".

You can just see yourself sitting there, can't you?

Heavens, you can taste that breakfast, feel those lashings of butter dribbling down your chin...

- **OPEN:** All year except Xmas.
- **ROOMS:** Three rooms, all en suite.
- **AVERAGE PRICE:** £18 per person sharing, £20 single.
No Extra Charges.
- **CREDIT CARDS:** No Credit Cards.

- **NOTES:**
High Tea served on request.
No Licence.
No Wheelchair Access.
Children – over 6 only.
Vegetarian breakfast available.
No Pets. Private Car Parking.
Chez Nous is signposted on the main N7 Dublin/Cork/Limerick road, a few miles north of Portlaoise. Coming from Dublin, keep an eye out for the sign on the right hand side of the road.

PRESTON HOUSE CAFÉ ⚆ⓡ
Alison & Michael Dowling
Abbeyleix
Co Laois
Tel: (0502) 31432/31662

Alison Dowling's cooking makes you feel good. Simple as that.

And in the Preston House Café, the noble stone building in the centre of Abbeyleix village which she and Michael Dowling have converted from an old Protestant boy's school into a restaurant with rooms, she has found the perfect place in which to make you feel good.

Mrs Dowling's cooking has always had this gift. For some years she ran Glebe House, a little hideaway where you could forget the rest of the world and immerse yourself in the sort of cooking that gave you an appetite the instant you saw it.

People fell in love with the place, with the food and the comfort, above all with Alison Dowling's affable and calming manner.

Well, for those who have missed it since Glebe House closed, and for those who have never experienced it, Preston House gives everyone a chance to encounter not just the sort of food that makes you feel smashing, but also that affable, amiable manner.

And Mrs Dowling's generous manner is an integral part of her cooking. This is true country cooking, virtuous, flavour-filled, the sort of thing that creates happiness.

She keeps her cooking straightforward, logical. Chicken fillets in a white wine sauce with rice; pan fried trout with a garden salad; a warm salad with Rudd's ham, the local Abbey Blue brie, walnuts and croûtons.

There are good open sandwiches of baked ham with mustard mayonnaise, or river trout with a fennel mayonnaise, wholemeal brown bread with cold roast chicken.

Dinner will offer tomato and basil soup; roast leg of lamb with redcurrant jelly; chicken with almonds and wholegrain mustard, these served with green runner beans and courgettes, then lemon ice cream or fruit charlotte pudding.

Simple comfort food which, in Mrs Dowling's hands, screams out, Try Me!

There are six cosy rooms in Preston House, and it is the sort of place you look forward to finding yourself in.

The fact that it is smack bang on the main Dublin to Cork road, and thus offers solace to car-addled folk who either need to grab something to eat, or else want to call a halt to the driving and stop for dinner and a place to stay, makes it a national treasure.

● **OPEN:** All year.
Kitchen open 10am-7pm Mon-Sun.
Dinner from 8pm Thur-Sat.
Sun lunch 1pm-2.30pm.
● **ROOMS:** Six rooms, all en suite.
● **AVERAGE PRICE:**
À la carte Lunch under £10.
Dinner over £20.
Sun lunch over £10.
● **CREDIT CARDS:** Visa, Access/Master.

● **NOTES:**
Wine Licence.
Children – welcome.
No Wheelchair Access.
In the centre of Abbeyleix, at the southern end of the village, on the main N7 Dublin to Cork road.

ROUNDWOOD HOUSE ◊
Frank & Rosemary Kennan
Mountrath
Co Laois
Tel: (0502) 32120

What might be grandiose in another place, another province, tends to remain unassuming, unforced, in County Laois.

Take a pub like Morrissey's in Abbeyleix, for example.

Were one to transport it to Dublin or Galway, even to Cork, and certainly to Bunratty, then it would quickly become a pickled tourist trap, somewhere famous for being famous.

In Abbeyleix, this extraordinary pub simply gets on with the business of serving drink, as it has done for decades, refusing to allow time to change it: there is still the old counter of foods, still the old biscuit tins, still the respect for a fine pint of stout which they have always pulled.

This modesty extends to Frank and Rosemary Kennan's Round-wood House, one of the most affectionately regarded places to stay in the entire country.

Elsewhere, it would become a staple of the glossy guidebooks. Here, in this modest county, it stays a secret, almost.

An air of lazy, pleasure-filled idyll pervades the house, creating a place so story-book super – with its commingling ducks and its horses, its wide rooms with tall windows, its slightly-knocked-about charm – that you might imagine yourself transported to some never-never land, a province straight from the pages of Janet and Allan Ahlberg.

It is all smiles and grins, cheekily unpretentious. Some folk don't fall for its modest, almost-eccentric charms, but these folk probably think the trouser press is the greatest invention of the century.

Rosemary Kennan's cooking is expert, soulful, flavour-addled, a lot of it coming from the Aga and boasting that maternal, careful care which makes the straightforward seem especially rejuvenating, a style which is also full of intriguing twists which her hungry mind adds to the repertoire of country house fare.

Breakfasts are scrumptious, and dinner a delight of modest, skillful food. The visitors' book, almost more than any other in the entire country, pays tribute to the Kennans' skill, their concern, their quiet savoir faire. You too will be queueing up to trump up superlative words of thanks.

- ● **OPEN:** All year.
- ● **ROOMS:** Six rooms, all en suite.
- ● **AVERAGE PRICE:** £35 per person sharing, £41 single.
10% discount for 2 nights.
No Service Charge.
- ● **CREDIT CARDS:**
Visa, Access/Master, Amex, Diners.

- ● **NOTES:**
Dinner for guests, £20, book by 4pm,
Sun lunch £12, for guests and non-residents if pre-booked.
Wine Licence.
No Wheelchair Access.
Children – high chairs, cots, babysitting.
Pets accommodated, but not in rooms.
Roundwood House is signposted from Mountrath, a few miles south of Portlaoise on the Limerick road.

JORDAN'S PUB & BISTRO ⊕ ℝ
Harry & Marian Jordan
Newry Street
Carlingford
Co Louth
Tel & Fax: (042) 73223

They are good restaurateurs, Harry and Marian. They describe their cooking as "parochial", but don't imagine that means they are narrow-minded or happy to plough a narrow furrow.

They aren't, and here "parochial" means simply that they have fine respect for local foods – Slieve Foy mushrooms, these served with a little puff pastry and a fine lime sauce; or Carlingford oysters, these with a wedge of lemon, or perhaps a warmed pesto or a good provençale, and some of their excellent breads, or perhaps a vegetable dish of local wild samphire, or a main course of Annagassan lobster.

If they are good restaurateurs, it is perhaps because they are fluent, confident cooks. Dinner may begin with an excellent leek and Cashel Blue tartlet, or a clever chicken and pork liver parfait, then a consoling bowl of carrot and parsnip soup, or, if you are lucky, their stunning curried parsnip soup, a bowl of sheer delight which is a definition of the soupmaker's art.

You might choose their signature dish of braised shank of lamb – one bite will show why it is their signature dish – or maybe pheasant on braised red cabbage, a fine chicken gremolata, or perhaps that gremolata with a baked darne of cod, or perhaps or a duo of smoked haddock and baked cod.

This is very real cooking, determined to coax out flavour, determined to offer food which is logical, local, satisfying.

Indeed, where other restaurants in Louth tend to interpret satisfaction as meaning the need to offer four types of potato dish, the Jordans know that satisfaction comes from soulful, smart cooking, and not from excess. Mind you, they do like scrummy desserts – steamed sticky ginger pudding with a butterscotch sauce, maybe a brandy sauce for an apple charlotte – but everything here is very well measured, well orchestrated.

Perhaps part of their success stems from the fact that they have not lost a jot of enthusiasm for the job. They alternate nights in the kitchen – Harry one night, Marian the next – with nights at front of house, and they are excellent at both. The rooms, in an old converted potato shed at rere of the restaurant, are just grand: spacious, calm, with terrific views.

- **OPEN:** 6.30pm-10pm Tue-Sun, 12.30pm-2.30pm Sun.
(Early menu summer months).
- **AVERAGE PRICE:** B&B £30 per person sharing.
Table d'hôte Dinner £21. Sun lunch £12.50
- **ROOMS:** Seven rooms, all en suite.
- **CREDIT CARDS:**
Visa, Access/Master, Amex, Diners.

- **NOTES:**
Full Bar Licence.
Children – welcome, cot and extra bed available.
Wheelchair Access.
In the centre of Carlingford.

CROOKEDWOOD HOUSE ⓑⓐ

Noel & Julie Kenny
Crookedwood
Mullingar
Co Westmeath
Tel: (044) 72165

Noel and Julie Kenny's restaurant occupies a vital role in the quixotic midlands of the country, where the flatlands of Dublin and Meath quickly expire in the rush of lake water, and the topographical ruggedness which signals that you are, suddenly, making your way into the west of the country.

Mr Kenny's skills are diverse and his cooking is richly sensuous. He trained for a time in Germany and, whilst some might consider this a distinctly ambiguous pedigree – rather like accusing some one of having a German sense of humour – Mr Kenny seems to have learnt there the ability to fuse powerful flavours with delicate ingredients.

You see this at work when he mixes pasta with shellfish – mussels with fettucine, maybe prawns laced with Pernod to accompany the starchy staple – and the delicate plainness of the pasta is greedily counterpointed by the sweet, punchy shellfish.

The Mitteleuropean influence comes right to the fore when he utilises the wonderful local venison, and serves it in a gulyas with that rare and disarming staple that is spatzle.

He will also, intriguingly, pair the game with wild duck in a red wine sauce, a rich and sinuous creation, and combine a honey-roasted pork steak with salmon in filo, serving it with two sauces for an unusual surf 'n' turfer.

But aside from these amusements, Noel Kenny steers a straight line through the classic dishes: grilled rack of lamb with a herb crust; fillet steak with wild mushrooms and a tarragon sauce; grilled Dover sole meuniere; supreme of chicken Kiev; a double fillet steak with mushrooms, straw potatoes and a bearnaise sauce.

This is clever cooking, with the intelligence used to achieve pure, comforting tastes. The sense of comfort which the Kennys want you to enjoy runs right through the evening in Crookedwood: service and ambience and comfort make for a memorable experience. The new rooms which they have added are a perfect complement to the house, and this is a lovely hideaway in the midst of lakelands.

● **OPEN:** 7pm-10pm Tue-Sat, 12.30pm-2.30pm Sun.
● **ROOMS:** Eight rooms, all en suite.
● **AVERAGE PRICE:**
Table d'hôte Dinner £19.50.
Sun lunch £12.50.
No Service Charge.
● **CREDIT CARDS:**
Visa, Access/Master, Amex, Diners.

● **NOTES:**
Full Licence.
Wheelchair Access (happy to help).
Children – welcome, cots, half portions.
Coming from Mullingar, turn right at the hospital on the road to Castlepollard, then drive to Crookedwood village. Turn right at the Wood pub, then one and a half miles further along you will see the house.

TEMPLE ⊕
Declan & Bernadette Fagan
Horseleap
Moate
Co Westmeath
Tel & Fax: (0506) 35118

Good food, good crack, good fun, is the trilogy of delights which the regulars of Temple appreciate.

But we can make a quartet of this trilogy of appetising delights, for this is someplace special to relax, a feature of the house which is pre-eminent for the Fagan family.

Temple itself is a fine farmhouse set amidst a substantial sheep and cattle farm, and enjoys the rather curious architectural addendum of a wing, on the left side of the house, which seems to have been imported from a castle.

Inside, decorations are subtle and effective, calming from the minute you step inside. Indeed, the house is only a few hundred yards from one of the busiest roads in the country, but once you turn off the N6 and move slowly up the driveway, you enter a world a million miles away from supercharged daily life. Turn off the road, and turn off the cares of the workaday world.

Declan and Bernadette give Temple an easy-going grace, which means it is very much the sort of place that, after one visit, you want to head back to, preferably with a clatter of your friends and your bevy of kids.

Indeed, you are likely to find, staying here, that many of the other guests have been here many, many times, and that these regulars adore the house party feel.

Mrs Fagan's cooking is a fine-tuned, well-understood cuisine paysanne: terrific meat cookery, in particular, but the care and concentration of a good cook is everywhere: lovely breakfasts, excellent light lunches which often have a vegetarian theme, crisp, soulful vegetables, smashing gooey desserts which bring dinner to a roistering conclusion.

Mrs Fagan takes pleasure in the preparation of food, and it shows, and the generosity implicit in her culinary efforts is echoed in everything about the house.

They welcome kids, cooking for those on diets and for vegetarians is excellent, and you can even ask for aromatherapy or Ki-massage to be arranged during their relaxation weekends, if you can cope with even more blissfulness.

- **OPEN:** All year.
- **ROOMS:** Four rooms, all en suite.
- **AVERAGE PRICE:**
B&B £25 per person sharing.
Set Dinner £16.
- **CREDIT CARDS:**
Visa, Access/Master.
- **NOTES:**
Wine Licence.
Children – welcome. Slide, other children to play with, lambs to feed (season permitting), cots, high chairs.
Signposted from the N6 Kinnegad/Galway road. One mile west of Horseleap and four miles east of Moate.

THE WINEPORT RESTAURANT ®
Ray Byrne & Jane English
Glassan
Athlone
Co Westmeath
Tel: 0902) 85466

You can't help but be knocked sideways by the charm of everyone at The Wineport. You can't help but be delighted by how hard they work, how keen they are to please, how determined they are that you should have a good time.

Ray and Jane orchestrate and organise a happy bunch and a happy place, their attention and devotion evident in each and every detail of The Wineport.

The result of their hard work is a simple conclusion.

Everybody loves it.

Young and old, rich and otherwise, couples and families, golfers, sailors, those who hate golf and sailing. It is a charming place, simple as that.

They provide menus for just about everyone: Brunch for late Sunday, with duck liver salad, cod fillet with a basil and pine nut sauce; buckwheat and vegetable pies, perhaps a traditional Sunday roast.

For the kids there will be ham 'n' mushroom pizza, small portions of soup, ice-cream cones.

For golfers there are late afternoon menus: steamed mussels; pan-fried sirloin steak; stir-fried chicken and vegetables.

For those who pursue good food without the interruption of needless sporting behaviour, the menu is welcomingly balanced: baked goat's cheese and oven-dried tomatoes with a walnut and herb vinaigrette; a terrine of smoked salmon with a yogurt and chive cream; sole on the bone stuffed with prawns and crabmeat; ravioli filled with spinach and cheese with a tomato and basil sauce finished with shavings of Parmesan.

For those who must watch the waits, there are healthy options: three bean soup with coriander; scallops in filo with a citrus and chive dressing; baked trout with tarragon, lemon juice and olive oil. Honest, achievable, fine tasting food.

The Wineport sits hard on the inner lakes of Lough Ree, and can even be reached by boat.

Inside, it is a democratic ideal, a charming all-hands-on-deck place, and a winning success.

● **OPEN:** 12.30pm-2.30pm Sun, 6pm-10pm Mon-Sun (open noon-10pm high season).
● **AVERAGE PRICE:** Lunch £10. Dinner £12.50-£25. No Service Charge.
● **CREDIT CARDS:** Visa, Access/Master, Amex, Diners.

● **NOTES:**
Full Licence.
Wheelchair Access (happy to help).
Children – welcome, special menus.
Recommended for Vegetarians.
3 miles north of Athlone, leave the by-pass at exit 4, towards Glassan.
Access by boat also.

FURZIESTOWN HOUSE ◎
Yvonne Pim
Tacumshane
Co Wexford
Tel: (053) 31376

Furziestown is no more than a cutely nice farmhouse, set way, way down here in the heel of the country. If it was run by professional folk with water in their veins and profits on their brains it would still be a fine retreat, at any time of the year.

But, happily, it is run by Yvonne Pim, and the intuitive thoughtfulness which Mrs Pim brings to everything, and Mrs Pim's care and concern for her guests, makes the house someplace special. Modest where-withal be damned! This is one of the most highly regarded places to stay in the country. Walk in the door and you feel welcome. You don't even need to give her half a chance, and Mrs Pim spoils you. Without even trying, you will find that you love it.

And you will love the food, which reflects not just an environmentally sensitive cook, but a cook whose feel for flavour is unwaveringly exact. You could say that this is because Mrs Pim lets the food speak for itself – what could be more natural than organic roast lamb served with garden herbs, steamed scarlet runner beans, broad beans in a light bechamel sauce, and roast potatoes? – and the answer is: nothing, of course. But most cooks don't realise that natural, sensible, seasonal food is best. Yvonne Pim does, and that is the treat that lies in store in Furziestown.

Menus for vegetarians are extra special – mushroom croustades on a bed of mixed greens, chick peas in spiced lentil and coconut sauce with mixed rice, and there are also dishes for vegans – carrot and apple salad, then sesame tofu with stir-fried vegetables and mixed rice with courgettes and cashews. Breakfasts are a joy.

● **OPEN:** Mar-Nov.
● **ROOMS:** Three rooms, all en suite.
● **AVERAGE PRICE:**
£16 per person, no single supplement.
Set Dinner £13. No Service Charge.
● **CREDIT CARDS:** No Credit Cards.

● **NOTES:**
Dinner for residents only £13 3-course,
£10 2-course, book previous day.
No Licence (bring your own).
No Wheelchair Access, but 2 downstairs bedrooms suitable for disabled.
Children – high chairs, cots.
Recommended for Vegetarians.
Follow signs from Tacumshane.

KELLY'S STRAND HOTEL ◎
Bill Kelly
Rosslare
Co Wexford
Tel: (053) 32114
Fax: (053) 32222

When we first stayed in Kelly's, we stayed only for one night when travelling for the Rosslare ferry. We admired many things about the hotel – the service, the food, the art, the friendliness, the profound sense of relaxation, and criticised others – the uniformity of the rooms, the lack of an early breakfast.

Even then, we were conscious that to criticise such an august institution was, for some, almost sacriligeous, because for the scores of thousands of people who go to Kelly's each and every year, this is a place which can do no wrong.

So were we wrong? Not in the criticism, perhaps, but we were wrong in failing to appreciate the modus of Kelly's. If there is a secret here, it lies in the name. Kelly's Resort Hotel. This is not a functional, overnight place. You come here to tune in and drop out, to vanish from normal workaday cares. Kelly's no longer takes bookings for single night stays, for its function has been even more precisely defined by Bill Kelly and his staff. This is a resort hotel. A place for holidays. A place to stay, and to enjoy yourself. And there are few better places in Ireland to do so.

Bill Kelly and his family are consummate people managers, so their staff are dedicated, devoted, and happy in their work. In the kitchen, Jim Aherne and his team are magnificent, a stupendous engine room of good food, brilliantly managed for such numbers of people as would make you swoon just to think of it.

And, finally, Bill Kelly has good taste. Just look at the wine list. Just look at the art collection. Intricately composed and assembled, his work shows a man who appreciates profoundly and who understands nuance and subtlety, a man who looks for the integrity and substance of the thing. And that is what you get at Kelly's; not a copy or a facsimile, not a replica or something ersatz, but the real thing.

● **OPEN:** Mar-Nov.
Restaurant open to non residents
1pm-2.15pm, 7.30pm-9pm Mon-Sun.
● **ROOMS:**
Ninety-nine rooms, all en suite.
● **AVERAGE PRICE:** Accommodation generally offered, and priced, weekly.
Summer rate, full board, £450 per person.
10% Service Charge.
Telephone for other seasonal rates.
Non residents Lunch £12. Dinner £20.95.
● **CREDIT CARDS:**
Visa, Access/Master, Amex, Diners.

● **NOTES:**
Many sports and beauty facilities, including heated swimming pool, massage, hairdressing and reflexology.
Full facilities for children, including creche.
Full Bar Licence.
Full Wheelchair Access.
No pets.
Signposted from the main Rosslare road.

McMENAMIN'S TOWNHOUSE ◈
Seamus & Kay McMenamin
3 Auburn Terrace, Redmond
Road, Wexford, Co Wexford
Tel: (053) 46442

If there is one single element which remains with you after a stay at Seamus and Kay McMenamins' friendly and efficacious house, it is the generosity which underpins everything they do.

Ask a question about this delightful town or the delightful county, and you will be told all you need to know, and likely a bit more besides.

State an affection for some particular breakfast dish – some fish, maybe, or a necklace of rum to ring around your porridge, or a particular type of bread – and it will be brought to life next morning, all the better to delight you.

Indeed, the staggering choice of foods available at breakfast is almost overwhelming in its largesse: a bumper of breads, fruits, juices, eggs anywhichway, steaming coffee and wake-up tea are arrayed before you.

Their hospitality is true and, just like some visitors from Down Under who described the breakfasts as "phenomenal", you may find that you stay rather longer than you planned.

- **OPEN:** All year (except Xmas).
- **ROOMS:** Six rooms, all en suite.
- **AVERAGE PRICE:**
£18.50 per person sharing.
No Service Charge.
- **CREDIT CARDS:** Visa, Access/Master.

- **NOTES:**
Will book restaurants locally. No Licence.
No Wheelchair Access.
Children – welcome, cot provided.
No pets.
Private Parking.
Opposite the railway station, in the centre of Wexford town.

SALVILLE HOUSE ✦
Jane & Gordon Parker
Enniscorthy, Co Wexford
Tel: (054) 35252

Salville is a quietly inspiring, quietly uplifting house set snug on a hill overlooking a wood which, in autumn time, sets into a honeycomb of deep greens and bright browns.

You become familiar with the wood because one of the finest features of Salville – if we overlook the excellent food they concoct at breakfastime and dinnertime, and the continuous, steady improvements which they have made to the house – is the extraordinary large windows which dominate each of the rooms. These vast vistas of glass allow cascades of light to shock you into action each morning when you peel back the window shutters.

This sense of light, and the vast volume of space which each room offers, is enough to make one almost giddy with a surfeit of freedom, that holiday freedom that animates the blood once one is out on the road.

It makes this sublime house slightly fey and feminine in character, almost spiritual. There really isn't anywhere else with the character of Salville.

- **OPEN:** All year.
- **ROOMS:** Five rooms, one en suite.
- **AVERAGE PRICE:** £17.50-£20 per person sharing, £20-£25 single.
No Service Charge.
- **CREDIT CARDS:** No Credit Cards.

- **NOTES:**
Dinner for residents, £15, if pre-booked.
No Licence (bring your own).
Wheelchair Access
(telephone to discuss details).
Children – welcome, cot.
Pets by arrangement.
Just off the N11 to Wexford – take the first left after the hospital, go up the hill to a T-junction then turn left and proceed for one third of a mile.

Lovely lunch

AVOCA HANDWEAVERS ®

Joanna Hill
Kilmacanogue
Co Wicklow
Tel: (01) 286 7466
Fax: (01) 286 2367

"I never had designs on being a cook", says Leylie Hayes who, with head chef Joanna Hill, is the mastermind behind the cooking in Avoca Handweavers.

The food is fun, and perfectly constructed. You look at the assembly of dishes at lunchtime, their sparkling integrity and appearance, and want to try everything.

And goodness but it is good: a bowl of roasted tomato and red pepper soup, which shows the fondness of this kitchen for sweet flavours. Ms Hill's fantastic piperade tart, the slice topped with a ring of tomato, and the stew of peppers and onions bound up with goat's cheese, this accompanied by roasted fennel and red pepper salad, and grated carrot and sesame seed salad with a sesame dressing.

Or sesame glazed chicken, perfectly executed, with potato salad in a yogurt and mint dressing, and a lovely crunchy mixture of cauliflower, broccoli and peanut salad, with a mustard dressing. Smashing food, food that draws in people from many miles around, day after day.

The synergy between the tastes – the goat's cheese in the tart with the vegetables, the heat of mustard with the broccoli and cauliflower, the clever splash of pesto in the soup – shows the very astute culinary thinking of Joanna Hill. And, on any given day, the place will be jumping, the buzz of people enjoying themselves, people who know they are on to a good thing.

The key to this discipline lies with constant enquiry. Ms Hayes travels widely, staff are allowed sabbaticals to travel and learn about new cuisines. The dread of dullness and repetition is thus kept at bay. And with this constant enquiry comes constant innovation.

They have opened a new food hall, paved an area out front of the restaurant which they will cover over, and meantime Joanna Hill's food moves ever onwards, upwards, on the hunt for sublimity and perfection.

"But we don't think we ever have it right", says Ms Hayes. "We are pumping money back into the business all the time, trying to make it better". Of all the things to admire about Avoca perhaps this hunger to improve is the finest attribute of this fine venture.

● **OPEN:** 9.30am-5.30pm Mon-Fri, 10am-5.30pm Sat-Sun.
Food served all day, last food orders 4.45pm.
● **AVERAGE PRICE:** Lunch £5.
● **CARDS:**
Visa, Access/Master.

THE OLD RECTORY ◎
Paul & Linda Saunders
Wicklow, Co Wicklow
Tel: (0404) 67048
Fax: (0404) 69181

In Linda Saunders, one meets a person who is something of an aleph of County Wicklow. A vital and essential asset to the town and the county, her character seems to sum up this delightful place – quietly complex, slightly reserved, but pretty bloody determined behind it all – and her effusive and intricate cooking is a perfect reflection of the strengths and delights of Wicklow.

She uses fine organic ingredients, grown locally, and this explains firstly why her food always has a vibrancy and freshness about it: it seems to reflect and express the sunshiney, youthful nature of the Wicklow hills.

To this, she brings a degree of invention and expressiveness, and an intellectual comprehension and understanding of the architecture of taste, which few other country house cooks can match. Indeed, this sense of complex but compatible flavouring in her food is reminiscent of the structure of a perfume, with alluring scents and mellifluous taste structures to be enjoyed both in main dishes and in their compatriot sauces: a warm terrine of salmon and sea trout will swim along with a green herb sauce, parsnips will pair off with red beans for a soup, whilst the elegant ruddiness of a carrot and cucumber tart will have the warm spice of marjoram underpinning it.

But there is more to Linda Saunders' skill than just the ability to conjure intricate tastes with skill. She also, bravely, can construct entire dinner menus to arrive at compatibility and complexity and, to celebrate the Wicklow Flower Festival, cooks a dauntingly daring ten course Floral Dinner: kale flower purses in filo; gazpacho ropjo with iced borrage blossoms; roast quail stuffed with apple, pine nut and sage flowers, a jamboree of tastes.

The extension of the dining room has gifted the Old Rectory with greater light, perfect for a cuisine of such delicacy, and Paul Saunders' intelligent collection of wines is terrifically promising. Rooms in the house are cosy, and whilst the Rectory is a good base for exploring Wicklow, you will likely find that you want to eat nowhere but here.

● **OPEN:** 29 Mar-26 Oct.
● **ROOMS:** Five rooms, all en suite.
● **AVERAGE PRICE:** £46 per person sharing, single supplement £23.
No Service Charge.
Dinner from £27.
● **CREDIT CARDS:**
Visa, Access/Master, Amex, Diners.

● **NOTES:**
Restaurant open to non residents
Sun-Thur 8pm, Fri-Sat 7.30pm-9pm, booking essential.
Wine Licence.
Wheelchair Access – one downstairs bedroom.
Children – welcome.
Recommended for Vegetarians.
No pets.
Enclosed Car Park.
30 miles south of Dublin (45 mins), on the left hand side of the road as you enter Wicklow town, heading South.

TINAKILLY HOUSE ◎ℝ
William & Bee Power
Rathnew, Co Wicklow
Tel: (0404) 69274

In a world of hotels where the anodyne and the anonymous, the bland and the bureaucratic, are the norm, Tinakilly House is a beacon to restore hope to the traveller's heart.

It is a shimmering edifice, which manages to combine all of those elements which animate the hotel of our dreams. There is the spit 'n' polish professionalism found in every detail of the operation, so it glides like a gleaming machine.

There is the upright, ridiculously-polite figure of William Power, who is seemingly available at every moment of the day to answer any query and set any matter to right, not just the manager, but the owner.

There are blazing fires, yawningly huge balconies and balustrades, and generous suites painted in rich, relaxing colours, as if Norman Rockwell had been called in to design the interiors.

And, vitally, there is the cooking.

For Tinakilly breaks with the norm of Irish hotel cooking in as much as John Moloney's work is inventive, seasonal and enormously enjoyable.

He concocts a rich, sumptuous meld of flavours, but if his food is grand, it is also wisely modern and light.

He will steam fillets of lemon sole and pair them with beurre blanc and dill. His fillet of beef with champ is enlivened by a thyme and black peppercorn jus.

He makes a demon warm chicken mousse and stuffs it with blue cheese, makes a perfect saffron cream for turbot. This is fine cooking, with ambition and ex-ecution working hand in hand.

Indeed, Mr Moloney's modernism is probably the only concession Tinakilly makes to a confection which is otherwise narcotically nostalgic.

Here in County Wicklow, in the polite, well-mannered county they call "The Garden of Ireland", Tinakilly House is a place of calm order, discipline and devotion.

"Ambience and service are first class", was how a correspondent summed up Tinakilly.

He might have added, "and so is everything else".

● **OPEN:** All year.
Restaurant open to non residents
12.30pm-2pm, 7.30pm-9pm Mon-Sun.
(Booking essential).
● **ROOMS:**
Twenty-six rooms, all en suite, three suites.
● **AVERAGE PRICE:**
B&B from £55-£70 per person, low season.
£63-£80 high season.
Lunch £17.50. Dinner £30.
No Service Charge.
● **CREDIT CARDS:**
Visa, Access/Master, Amex, Diners.

● **NOTES:**
Open for Xmas.
Breakfast In Bed a feature of the hotel.
Children – welcome.
Full Bar Licence.
Signposted from Rathnew, and just south of the village.

MUNSTER

from East coast
to

West coast
via

the Golden Vale

BARRTRÁ SEAFOOD RESTAURANT ⊛
Paul & Theresa O'Brien
Lahinch, Co Clare
Tel: (065) 81280

The Barrtrá is such a sweet, good family operation, such a cloisteringly comfortable, logical little restaurant, that it is well nigh irresistible.

Paul does front of house, Theresa cooks, and at busy times their daughters lend a hand and put together the desserts. The diners sit in what is, effectively, a room of the O'Brien's house, looking out at Liscannor Bay, a heartbreakingly beautiful vista. If there is a classic summertime restaurant, with all the holidaytime clichés – friendly food, good service, fine wines, the romance of looking out at the sea as the sun sets – then this is it.

Of course, like any dream, it is founded in the rock-solid realities of hard work. Theresa is constantly innovating and introducing new dishes – home-smoked shark sausage; prawns in hot olive oil with smoked garlic; oysters with garlic butter – and they constantly refine and revise the local classics – baked crab; hot buttered lobster; Burren lamb, duck with port sauce.

The vegetables are grown organically, the wines are an interesting and diverting selection, and this is the sort of little restaurant you dream of stumbling across when on holiday, a little oasis of delight.

● OPEN: 12.30pm-2.30pm Mon-Sun, 6pm-10pm Mon-Sat. (Closed weekdays off season, closed mid Jan-Mar).

● AVERAGE PRICE: Lunch under £10. Sun lunch under £15. Dinner £16.50-£19.
● CREDIT CARDS: Visa, Access/Master, Amex, Diners.

● NOTES:
Wine Licence.
No Wheelchair Access.
Children – welcome, early evenings only.
Recommended for Vegetarians.
Signposted from the Lahinch-Milltown Malbay Road.

CAHERBOLANE FARMHOUSE ⊛⊛
Brid & Patricia Cahill
Corofin, Co Clare
Tel: (065) 37638

Both in her personality and in the confident cooking she delivers in the surrealistically unlikely setting of Caherbolane Farmhouse, near Corofin, Patricia Cahill leaves you in no doubt: she knows what she wants to do, and she knows how to do it.

A very pure streak of perfectionism runs through her work, and her ambition is helped by the fact of cooking in Caherbolane, for it is, in fact, the intimately small. sitting room of the farmhouse, and in evening time is host to no more than five tables.

Cooks like Patricia Cahill understand those flavours and savours which are best at cranking our pleasure dials to the max. She does this with stupendously simple things – a floury potato steamed to utter perfection; mashed turnips with a hint of cinnamon stirred in; crunchy, creamy cabbage, and the confident nature of her technique means that dinner becomes a solid sender of good tastes.

Alongside easy-going starters such as melon and avocado with a mint dressing, there could be ravioli stuffed with nuts and served with a pesto sauce.

Main courses like sirloin of beef with a prune and pepper sauce, and veal with a blue cheese sauce, are pristine examples of the arts of livestock, butchering and cooking. Desserts may be a thunderously good champagne parfait or a simple coffee crème caramel.

You would pay the earth for this, yet it costs half nothing and as the farmhouse is unlicenced, you can bring your own wine. The rooms upstairs are comfortable and welcoming.

● **OPEN:**
Easter-Oct 7.30pm-9.30pm Mon-Sun.
● **ROOMS:** Four rooms, sharing two shower rooms.
● **AVERAGE PRICE:** B&B £15. Dinner £16.
● **CREDIT CARDS:** No Credit Cards.

● **NOTES:**
No Licence. Bring Your Own Wine.
Children – welcome, special menus.
No pets. Three miles outside Corofin on the road to Gort.

FERGUS VIEW
The Kelleher family
Kilnaboy Corofin, Co Clare
Tel: (065) 37606

Mary Kelleher's house is a landmark for hospitality – that lovely, easy,

capable, Clare hospitality – and for fine, fine food.

"We're interested in food and cooking", says Mrs Kelleher, which stands as the understatement of this and any other year. This lady can cook, a subtle, domestic style which knocks your socks off.

Dinner at Fergus View exploits Mrs Kelleher's interest and her expertise translates into delectable, delicious food: a perfect mushroom crêpe; some river trout cooked en papilotte and elegantly served; a glorious potato gratin made with Kilnaboy cheese; tiny new potatoes; a purée of spinach, then pear frangipane and fine coffee. Heavenly, or what?

Breakfast, meantime, offers another feast: crêpes with kiwi fruit and maple syrup; smoked kippers with tomato; a bumper breakfast of bacon with true free-range eggs.

The housekeeping in Fergus View is meticulous and the rooms extra comfortable: this is a homely house.

● **OPEN:** Easter-Oct.
● **ROOMS:** Six rooms, five en suite.
● **AVERAGE PRICE:**
B&B £15-£17. Single Supplement £6.
Dinner £14.50, 6.30pm, book by noon.
● **CREDIT CARDS:**
No Credit Cards.

● **NOTES:**
Wine Licence.
Children - welcome, cot, high chair, babysitting.
No Pets.
The house is two miles north of Corofin on the left hand side of the road.

ADÈLE'S ⊗ⓇⒶ✪
Adèle & Simon Connor
Main Street, Schull
Co Cork
Tel: (028) 28459

Adèle's Bakery in Schull is much much more than simply a bakery.

It would, let's face it, be enough if the Connor's establishment served nothing other than the crumbling croissants, the petite sourdough loaves, carrot cakes that are altogether venal, crusty white loaves and comforting cottage pies. But there is more: lunch offers salads, omelettes and delightful filled ciabatta loaves – the olivy ciabatta rolls made by Adèle.

Then, during the evening Adèle's son, Simon, takes over the kitchen, and the bakery becomes a restaurant.

The simplicity of the dishes which Simon Connor prepares in Adèle's – poached salmon with a black pepper vinaigrette on mung bean sprouts; spaghetti with parsley pesto, or that spaghetti served with peppers and mushrooms; tagliatelle in an anchovy cream; angel hair pasta with mussels in a spicy tomato sauce; pappardelle with chicken liver and marjoram – doesn't hint at the increasing confidence with which he has begun to cook.

Mr Connor has the considerable benefit of being self-taught, so there is no nonsensical strait-jacket of technique tying down his imagination.

He manages to prepare correct food which never concedes a complexity of flavours: it looks simple, but the tastes are involved, and thereby involving. Something like tagliatelle with anchovy cream will manage to be rich, sinuous, intense, satisfying, inspired, and yet the ingredients could not be more obvious.

The teaming of everything, from pasta to sauce, from dish to dressing, from beat-box atmosphere to hip-hop staff, from rare French country wines to spectacular Italian specialities, is splendid.

Adèle's is a carefree, romantic, youthful space, somewhere you come to enjoy yourself.

And, by heck, do you enjoy yourself, with the comfort of knowing that there are four simple rooms upstairs where the final guise of Adèle's comes into your scheme of things.

This converted bank building becomes a B&B, with all those sensational breads to look forward to next morning.

● **OPEN:** 9.30am-10.30pm Mon-Sun (check out of high season).
Closed Nov-Apr.
(Open three weeks at Xmas).
● **ROOMS:**
Four rooms, sharing one shower-room.
● **AVERAGE PRICE:** B&B £12.50.
Lunch £3-£7. Dinner £8-£15.
No Service Charge, apart from parties of six or more, 10%.
● **CREDIT CARDS:** Visa, Access/Master.

● **NOTES:**
Wine Licence.
Wheelchair Access, but not to toilets.
Children – high chairs and half portions.
Vegetarian options always available.
At the top of the hill on Main Street in Schull.

AHERNE'S
SEAFOOD BAR ⓡⓐ
The Fitzgibbon family
163 North Main Street, Youghal,
Co Cork
Tel: (024) 92424, Fax: (024) 93633

There is a happy sense of timelessness about Aherne's.

That timelessness may be created by the fact that it is currently the third generation of Fitzgibbons who run this handsome place. But it may, equally, be the true sense of professionalism and a seriousness of purpose which the family espouse and practice, which makes the place ever-enduring.

This seriousness of purpose manifests itself as a determination to do things properly. This applies whether that is with the simple food cooked in the bar – you must try that mighty dish where smoked salmon and potatoes are gratinéed together, not to mention the great prawns in garlic butter and their fabulous seafood chowder – or in the cloistering, plump enfolds of the dining room, when David Fitzgibbon's fish cookery is given free and full rein – pan-fried scallops, monkfish and prawns in a coral sauce; Youghal Bay lobster thermidor; poached brill and prawns in Chablis; grilled sole on the bone.

This is very classic fish cooking, of course, and Aherne's follows a strict culinary code: If it ain't broke, don't fix it. The fish and shellfish dishes arrive with the classic accompaniments ever on hand, and they carry a near-certain rate of success.

Indeed, a success in Aherne's may gift you with some of the finest fish cooking it is possible to enjoy anywhere in the world, and you will go away and find that you, like so many others before you, have turned into a Cod Bore, or a Brill Bore, anxious to tell all and sundry about that fabulous fillet you enjoyed, that soulful shellfish which knocked you sideways, anxious to get the chance to explain to someone how bewitching it was. Sure, just wait 'till you tell them, they won't believe it...

● **OPEN:** All year.
Food served 12.30pm-2.15pm,
6.30pm-9.30pm Mon-Sun.
(Bar meals 11am-10pm Mon-Sun).
● **ROOMS:** Ten rooms, all en suite.
● **AVERAGE PRICE:**
B&B £50 per person sharing.
Lunch £15. Dinner £25.
Bar meals from £5.
10% Service Charge.
● **CREDIT CARDS:**
Visa, Access/Master, Amex, Diners.

● **NOTES:**
Full Pub Licence.
Wheelchair Access (incl. disabled toilet).
Children – welcome.
At the Waterford end of town.

ANNIE'S ⓡ
Dano & Annie Barry
Main Street, Ballydehob, Co Cork
Tel: (028) 37292

Annie Barry has the bestest, nicest, manner of any restaurant owner in the country. Her pacific nature with kids is legendary – Mrs Barry herself, of course, is too modest to agree with this – but she works her spell on adult kids with the same surreptitious ease, and quickly has you boggle-eyed and goo-goo with anticipation for the treat that is dinner in Annie's.

The restaurant is just a single room, with tables in multiples of pairs, nice and bright in summertime if you choose an early evening dinner, with drinks across the road in Levis's pub while you choose from the menu before Annie comes over to fetch you. Mr Barry doesn't try to do too much – and doesn't need to do too much – to coax the very best from his good ingredients.

The most preparation a piece of Sally Barnes's super smoked salmon ever needs is a squidge of lemon; with scallops as big and fat and coral-clawed as the ones you find in here, then a cream and white wine sauce may almost seem superfluous, but the sauce will be generous and precise, as generous and precise as an apricot sauce around a piece of finely roasted duck. The cooking may be light in execution, but it is deep in savour.

Right down to the very simple things – some luscious boiled spuds which you gobble up with the appetite of someone who has been hacking turf all day long, some baked cod or maybe – this is the regular's choice – a super-duper steak and some fab chips – Annie's gets it right. The temperament of this little place never changes, and never needs to, for who would tamper with a classic?

● **OPEN:** 6.30pm-9.30pm Tue-Sat
(always check winter opening hours).

● **AVERAGE PRICE:**
Dinner £22. No Service Charge.
● **CREDIT CARDS:** Visa, Access/Master.

● **NOTES:**
Wine Licence.
Wheelchair Access to restaurant but not to toilets.
Children – welcome, but no facilities.
Recommended for Vegetarians provided you give notice.
In the centre of Ballydehob, across from Levis's pub.

ASSOLAS HOUSE ✿✿✪
Joe & Hazel Bourke
Kanturk, Co Cork
Tel: (029) 50015, Fax: (029) 50795

That fine food writer, Annie Bell, wrote of the cooking in Assolas House, that "It is the absence of vanity in Hazel Bourke's cooking that makes it special: her 'dare to be simple' approach allows ingredients to speak for themselves".

No one has better described the work of this modest and most singular cook, and it is that aphoristic phrase "absence of vanity", which is the keynote. Hazel Bourke's food is confoundedly simple, and devastatingly delicious, so much so that if you were forced to find a single cook whose skill in the kitchen summons forth those flavours and tastes which one thinks of as quintessentially Irish, it is likely that it would be Mrs Bourke who would be summoned to summon forth those flavours.

She achieves this largely because she totally avoids the confections and artifices which seduce so many chefs. You can stay here for a week, and there will not be a single thing which you will eat which will overreach either itself, or the abilities of the kitchen.

Dinner menus from a few days in the middle of summer included dishes such as grilled black sole on the bone with garden herbs; fillet of brill baked in a wild mushroom crust on a delicate mustard sauce; grain-fed pigeon in red wine sauce; cream of garden peapod soup with croûtons, twice-baked Ardrahan cheese soufflé; oyster soup.

None of these dishes are new, but in Mrs Bourke's hands they are born anew each night. "Cooking? That's when things taste of themselves", wrote the great food sage Curnonsky. No one, but no one, is better at unravelling and unveiling the natural tastes of foods than Hazel Bourke.

And no one is better at orchestrating the service of these dishes than Joe Bourke, and nowhere is as nice a place in which to enjoy these dishes than Assolas. Be careful however: for there may be moments here of such utter bliss, that you will feel you shall surely expire from pleasure.

● **OPEN:** Mar-Nov. 7pm-8.30pm Mon-Sun (non-residents booking essential).
● **AVERAGE PRICE:**
B&B from £50-£67 per person sharing.
Dinner £28.
No Service Charge (tipping not expected).
● **CREDIT CARDS:**
Visa, Access/Master, Amex.

● **NOTES:**
Full Licence.

Wheelchair Access to restaurant but not toilets.
Children – welcome, cotes, high chair.
On the Mallow to Killarney road, follow signs to Kanturk. Four-and-a-half miles before Kanturk you will see signs for Assolas House.

BALLYMAKEIGH HOUSE ⊘
Mrs Margaret Browne
Killeagh, Co Cork
Tel: (024) 95184

For anyone who has ever wondered what makes one place to stay better than another, for anyone who wonders just what you have to do, and what kind of place you have to run, in order to get included in a Bridgestone Guide, may we offer the following as an example of just what you need to do to gain not only our approval, but the approval of both visitors to Ireland and the natives themselves.

"My girlfriend and I travelled to Ireland for Valentine's Weekend and we had a whopping great time at this gem of a place", writes a Mr McKenna, from London — no relation, we hasten to add — before hitting overdrive in order to describe Margaret Browne's Ballymakeigh House.

"The house was so welcoming and warm with every comfort one would need, big fires, fresh flowers, crisp linen, rich and warm décor. The warm welcome even extended right through to the tea leaves".

All of this is completely true, utterly unarguable, though we're not too sure about the tea leaves bit. But there is more. "The food deserves a special mention. It all tasted so fresh, wonderful and light. I just happened to mention one morning that I love hot oysters and roast duck and that night that was exactly what Mrs Browne served to us for dinner – all at a very reasonable cost".

Unsurprisingly, Mr McKenna concludes: "I shall definitely return there again".

Well, he would be crazy not to, wouldn't he?

And, if you have not discovered the cossetting and the comforting which is intrinsic, endemic and almost rampant in Mrs Browne's celebrated house, then we would have to reckon that you must be slightly crazy.

And once you have been there, you will know exactly what it is that makes one place better than another, and just what it is that makes Ballymakeigh someplace better than most.

● **OPEN:** All year.
● **ROOMS:** Five rooms, all en suite.
● **AVERAGE PRICE:**
£20 per person sharing, £25 single.
No Service Charge.
Dinner £20.
● **CREDIT CARDS:** No Credit Cards.

● **NOTES:**
Dinner for residents only, book by 5.30pm.
Wine Licence.
No Wheelchair Access.
Children – high seat, cot, babysitting.
Killeagh is between Castlemartyr and Youghal on the N25: watch for the sign to the house, beside the Old Thatch pub.

BALLYMALOE HOUSE ⊗⊗
Ivan & Myrtle Allen
Shanagarry, Midleton, Co Cork
Tel: (021) 652531, Fax: (021) 652021

Myrtle Allen' s philosophy of food in Ballymaloe House is durable, homespun, simple.

First, a country house hotel must encourage a circle of producers around and about you to produce the best foods they can, and you must support them as best you can.

Keep everything local and, thereby, enjoy the benefit of foods which express themselves in terms of the micro-climate in which they are produced and reared.

Secondly, try to be as self-sufficient as you can: grow your own spuds, make your own chutneys, produce as much of the food you need through your own endeavours.

Then, when it comes to the cooking of this food, do it from scratch, and do it with ingredients as pristinely fresh as possible. No egotism must blunt the edge of the cooking: you just allow the food to speak of and for itself.

Then, when it comes to serving the food, do it simply, but courteously and as graciously as you can, with easy, spontaneous dialogue between customer, waiting staff and cook, a culinary conversation.

In 1995, Myrtle Allen ceded the hands-on stewardship of her kitchen to Rory O'Connell, a daunting succession to contemplate.

But Rory understands well the great Ballymaloe verities – superb soups, great pâté maison in the style of a terrine of foie gras, good salads, the splendid, soulful breads – and these dishes are as well crafted and as completely realised as ever.

With time, he will surely unearth a more philosophical and more resonant style with his food, which is technically assured but still very much the cooking of a young man, a fact which can, curiously, make his work seem more conservative and cautious than the lively improvisations and inventions of a senior stateswoman of the kitchen like Myrtle Allen.

The rooms in the restaurant are as splendid and womb-welcoming as ever, the art collection – Cooke, Scott, Jellett, Yeats – gifted with an agelessness and vigour that makes it more luminescent with each visit.

● **OPEN:** All year.
Buffet Lunch 1pm.
Dinner 7pm-9pm Mon-Sun
(buffet dinner Sun).
● **AVERAGE PRICE:**
B&B £65 per person sharing.
Lunch £16.50. Dinner £30.
No Service Charge.
Visa, Access/Master, Amex, Diners.
● **CREDIT CARDS:**
Visa, Access/Master, Amex, Diners.

● **NOTES:**
Full Licence.
Wheelchair Access to restaurant but not easily to toilets.
Children – high chairs, reductions for under 9yrs.
Recommended for Vegetarians.
Ballymaloe House is signposted from the N25 Cork-Waterford road, between Midleton and Castlemartyr, and in Midleton.

BALLYVOLANE HOUSE ◎
Merrie & Jeremy Green
Castlelyons, Rathcormack,
Fermoy, Co Cork
Tel: (025) 36349
Fax: (025) 36781

The area of east County Cork where we find Merrie and Jerrie's Ballyvolane House is swollen with a meandering obliqueness, suffused with a relaxed and relaxing air of procrastination, cocooned in nicely lazy sort of country.

Ballyvolane sits comfortably and happily on the hillside at Castlelyons, quietly luxurious amongst quietly luxurious grounds, snuggled in amidst the infernal charm of County Cork.

Inside, the house is full of the right sort of burnished mahogany, and while portraits of long-gone ancestors glare down at you from the walls, anything ominous in their gaze is dissipated by the air of giddy, giggly fun which swaddles everyone staying here.

The dinner party cooking, the bright fires, the gin and tonics: it's so appropriate it deserves to be satirised.

Whilst there is much to admire everywhere throughout the house, the titanically deep baths in the front bedrooms are so gargantuan and epic they actually have to be stepped up to before you sink into.

These are the rooms to go for: the others are excellent, but perhaps not so much fun, and being merry is the modus vivendi of Ballyvolane, a place where formality surrenders to warm feelings of comfort and humour.

● **OPEN:** All year except Xmas.
● **ROOMS:** Six rooms, five en suite, one with private bathroom.
● **AVERAGE PRICE:** £35-£45 per person sharing, £10 single supplement. Dinner £22.50.
No Service Charge.
● **CREDIT CARDS:**
Visa, Access/Master, Amex.

● **NOTES:**
Dinner for guests only 8pm, book by noon.
Wine Licence.
Wheelchair Access.
Children – high chairs, cots, babysitting.
Pets welcome.
From Fermoy take the N8, and go through Rathcormac. After quarter of a mile turn left at the river Bridge. Follow four signs to the house.

BLAIR'S COVE RESTAURANT ®
Philippe & Sabine De Mey
Durrus, Co Cork
Tel: (027) 61127

People adore Blair's Cove. Indeed, there are few other restaurants in Ireland which can inspire and provoke the trembling announcements of true love which fans of Philippe and Sabine de Mey's handsome space will shamelessly proclaim. Mecca. Manna. Magnificent. Once they start, they simply cannot stop.

And it is easy to see why. The location is stunning – with views right out across Dunmanus Bay. The room is simply gorgeous – a converted barn with an arching ceiling and with a meat-grilling fire set on a podium at the far end. The dishes of the evening are written on a blackboard.

The centrepiece of the dining room is the huge array of hors d'oeuvres in the centre of the room, from which you choose to begin dinner. These can be quite fabulous: buttery pâtés; sweet and sour marinated herrings; some slender slices of good smoked salmon; a pair of lush oysters, the fine pickled vegetables, on and on it goes.

The main dishes work best when as simple as possible: you can't improve on char-grilled tuna, a fine casserole of venison with a venison sausage, perfect grilled lamb, maybe an entrecote with a fine bearnaise sauce. Simple, heavenly, and desserts continue the magic.

Service can be a little too relaxed at times, but oftentimes, with all this bliss going on, you scarcely notice its occasional shortcomings.

● **OPEN:** Mar-Nov, 7.30pm-9.30pm Tue-Sat (open Mon, Jul and Aug).
● **AVERAGE PRICE:** Dinner £25.
10% Service Charge.
● **CREDIT CARDS:**
Visa, Access/Master, Amex, Diners

● **NOTES:**
Restaurant Licence.
Wheelchair Access to restaurant but not to toilets.
Children – high chairs and half portions.
One Vegetarian main course served each evening.
One-and-a-half miles from Durrus on the Durrus-Goleen/Barleycove road: look for the gateway on the right-hand side.

BOW HALL ⊛
Dick & Barbara Vickery
Castletownshend,
Co Cork
Tel: (028) 36114

You meet Barbara Vickery and you think to yourself: this woman has just walked out of a kiddies' book. There she is, bow-tie bright, with those kind, kiddy-absorbing eyes, a little bundle of thoughtfulness and concern, and you think to yourself: why did we only book for three days! I don't want to leave!

Parting from Bow Hall is, truly, such sweet sorrow. But let's not think about the sorrow. Let's concentrate on the sweetness.

There are only three bedrooms in this fabulous house, and of course they all have names: the Apricot Room, the Toffee Room and the Oak Apple Room. The style mixes Shaker with a nod to the Arts & Crafts school, and it is an intensely family home: lots of wedding portraits and family snaps lining the walls, some nifty Oscar Peterson buzzing away in the background, a sitting room and library which looks like it has just walked out of a Frank Capra movie. Super cosy.

Mrs Vickery's breakfast muffins are already quietly famous, and one soft sweet mouthful will explain just why. She also makes a dynamite sausage, and light pancakes drizzled with maple syrup, and she cuddles your kid whilst you eat and chat to the other guests. And at some epiphanous moment, you will say to yourself: "Why, this is just like a kiddies' book story, and I am in it!" And so you are, so you are.

● **OPEN:** All year, except Xmas.
● **ROOMS:** Three double rooms, all with private bathrooms.
● **AVERAGE PRICE:**
B&B £30 per person sharing.
Dinner £20.
No Service Charge.
● **CREDIT CARDS:** No Credit Cards.

● **NOTES:**
Dinner for guests only.
No Wheelchair Access.
Children – high chair, cot.
No Pets.
In Castletownshend village centre, on the right hand side as you drive down the street.

CHEZ YOUEN ⊛
Youen Jacob
Baltimore, Co Cork
Tel: (028) 20136

It is in the luxurious, classical, educated richness of his sauces that we can locate Youen Jacob's easy, expert affinity with his craft.

An emulsion of pristine, slurpy mayonnaise in which to dunk your shellfish platter. A hollandaise of angelic lightness under a fillet of salmon. Cream with green peppercorns for roasted beef. With each dish, through the course of a dinner in Chez Youen, the sauce is as essential as the principal ingredient.

Indeed, with fish and shellfish, it can seem that the sauce is truly the star, the real performer on a stage otherwise set by the fish. It is simple food, classic French food, and it is perfectly done. At lunchtime the fish and shellfish and sauces marry so well with a bottle of Muscadet, the richness of one counterpointed by the mineral sharpness of the other, that you might just forget that there is any work to be done in the rest of the day. When you get around to eating some tarte tatin, the best tarte tatin in your life, you wish the crumbly, intensity could last forever.

The music is always good, contributing to the hedonistic vitality of the restaurant, the atmosphere agreeably unpretentiousness, and there is great, great fun to be had.

● **OPEN:** Easter-Sept, noon-2.30pm, 6.30pm-10.30pm.
● **AVERAGE PRICE:** Lunch £12.50. Dinner £21.50-£32.
No Service Charge.
● **CREDIT CARDS:**
Visa, Access/Master, Amex, Diners.

● **NOTES:**
Re-opens briefly for Xmas season.
Wine Licence.
Wheelchair Access
(1 step to restaurant, no access to toilet).
Children – welcome.
In centre of Baltimore village, overlooking the bay.

CLIFFORD'S & MICHAEL'S BISTRO ◐ ✪
Michael & Deirdre Clifford
18 Dyke Parade, Cork
Co Cork
Tel: (021) 275333

Clifford's Restaurant – Although he is an exceptionally shy and reserved man, there is a thoroughly unreserved and lush savouring for food, and for the creativity of cooking, pulsing through Michael Clifford's veins.

"I scoffed the semolina and even the tapioca, but my favourite treat then was toast cut thick and spread with good beef dripping. The jellied meat juices seeped through into the soft centre and liquified pleasantly against the tongue: to this day I am ready to put in a good word for my favourite". These words, from his first book of recipes are the measure of the man, and the measure of his food: deliciousness, at all costs.

His cooking strikes an original and exquisite balance between competing disciplines: whilst it is sumptuous and comforting, it is based on relatively simple ingredients; his work is cosmopolitan, yet never happiest than when working with something grown and produced as close to the restaurant as possible. His food is modern in style and technique, but he can manage to evoke a taste that seems age-old and yet – and this is vital – he avoids any sense of that dread nostalgia which so restricts Irish cuisine.

His improvisations with Edward Twomey's Clonakilty Black Pudding includes one dish where the pudding meets with blinis and a purée of mushrooms, and another which intriguingly marries pudding, a poached egg, cabbage and smoked kassler. His inventiveness never rests: breast of wood pigeon with glazed celeriac in its own juices; grilled scallops with an aubergine mousse; fillet of beef with braised salsify and a rich Fleurie sauce.

Indeed, all of Mr Clifford's

cooking, it seems, returns to that boyhood memory: warm, tactile tastes which melt and liquify, which sustain and delight. This romance with the whole business of cooking and running a restaurant makes Clifford's one of the most enjoyable places to eat in Ireland, for his staff are hopelessly happy in their work, and Michael's wife Deirdre augments the chef's shyness with her bubbly confidence.

Michael's Bistro – A restaurant should present a challenge: a bistro must present comfort. A restaurant should supply an excitement: a bistro must supply the familiar.

Happily, in Michael's Bistro, you need only push back the glass-inlaid doors, step onto the floorboards, and your heart breathes in all that we understand in bistro.

The food complements the concept perfectly. A bowl of cabbage soup floats on a chicken stock of perfect lightness and pointedness; cauliflower in a beer batter, with a tomato and garlic sauce, shows the fine tuning of sweet flavours, the florets crisp and fresh, the sauce was deliciously sympathetic.

With the signature dish of Irish Stew, the dish is, effectively, deconstructed, the ingredients taken apart and then re-assembled into a plate of food so earthy and generous that it seems to answer a craving in the soul rather than a simple craving of the appetite.

The pieces of lamb with their deep muttony savour are arrayed on one side, the soft cubes of potato, carrot, turnip and parsnip are on the other and ribbons of cabbage in the centre are sprinkled with pearl barley. A delicate soup of puréed vegetables lies underneath, and even with a touch of cream to finish the dish, the stew is light, full of supple flavours that are hugely satisfying.

With baby chicken, the fowl is roasted, then split, and a tumble of root vegetables acts as a stuffing, with a tarragon cream sauce underneath. Desserts are classic, and quite fab: a choux case filled with a Bailey's cream on a chocolate sauce and a fresh fruit pastry tartlet had perfect pastry, perfect custard. There is no better place in which to enjoy spuds and pearl barley, beef and cabbage, all the timeless aristocrats of the bistro.

● **OPEN:** Clifford's – 12.30pm-2.30pm, 7pm-10.30pm Tue-Sat.
Michael's Bistro – noon-3pm, 6pm-10.30pm Tue-Sat.
● **AVERAGE PRICE:**
Clifford's Lunch £11.50. Dinner £27.
Michael's Bistro – meals under £15.
No Service Charge.
● **CREDIT CARDS:**
Visa, Access/Master, Amex, Diners.

● **NOTES:**
Full Licence. No Wheelchair Access.
Children – welcome, but no facilities.
Special vegetarian menu offered in Clifford's after consultation with the chef, varied vegetarian options available in Michael's Bistro.
Both restaurants are a minute's walk from Jury's Hotel: turn left, then right and at the first set of traffic lights you will see them, side by side, on the corner.

CORTHNA LODGE ⊗
Loretta & Herbert Strickner
Schull, Co Cork
Tel: (028) 28517

A mile or so outside the vivacious village of Schull, a place which has a strong claim to be the food capital of Ireland and a place which, in season, stakes more than a claim to be the social capital of the country, Loretta and Herbert Strickner's Corthna Lodge exhibits all the grace notes of a house where guests are destined to be comprehensively cared for.

The gentleness and sweetness of Loretta and Herbert themselves is so understated that you can almost take it for granted, but stay here for a few days, however, and the attentive, tippy-toe air concern with which they do everything just compounds the pleasure of being here, as do the delicious breakfasts – steaming coffee, fresh eggs and bread, handmade cheese from Gubbeen farm just down the hill – all of it setting up so well the ripe promise of the day to come.

The evident care in the design of the rooms in this modern house, with their pastelly comfort and well-mannered charm, makes them cosy and comfortable, especially so when the wind is whipping about outside, as it is liable to do on this hill just south of Schull, as soon as summer fades and autumn begins. Corthna's skill is to combine the features of a special place – calm comfort, warm welcome, careful cooking – and to bundle them into a gift for the guest.

● **OPEN:** Apr-Nov.
● **ROOMS:** Six rooms, all en suite.
● **AVERAGE PRICE:** £20 per person sharing £25 single. No Service Charge.
● **CREDIT CARDS:** No Credit Cards.

● **NOTES:**
No restaurant
(but can book plenty in the locality).
No Licence.
Laundry Service available, from £5.
Wheelchair Access. Children – welcome.
Pets accommodated.
Three minutes drive, just outside Schull, driving towards Crookhaven, the house is signposted to the right.

DUNWORLEY COTTAGE RESTAURANT ⊗⊕
Katherine Noren
Dunworley, Butlerstown, Co Cork
Tel: (023) 40314

For those who love Katherine Noren's Dunworley Cottage Restaurant, it is unimaginable to consider that there might be other folk who would not regard this sacred shrine as one of the greatest restaurants in the country. They cannot conceive of people who do not, indeed, see it as one of the most singular restaurants in the north of Europe, a wild card, a one-off.

The disciples of Dunworley point eagerly and hungrily to its protean perfection; they go quiet with awe at the purity of taste which every morsel of the food Asa Helmerson cooks exhibits so perfectly; they go wide-eyed in explanation at the elemental wildness in which the restaurant is located, and how this is so decisive and important an influence on the foods which Mrs Noren collects and cooks. If there should, ideally, be a dialogue between every restaurant and the environment from which it sources and secures its foodstuffs, then Dunworley expresses that dialogue with the finesse of a Shakesperian ode.

Dunworley hand-raised pork is peerless; the veal used in the blanquette is surely one of the greatest things you have ever eaten in your life; the smoked salmon from Frank Hedermann can have a strong-willed stomach weak with delight; the cured salmon with some salmon roe in the cream is staggering; the smoked mussels seem out-of-this-world with their ether-ealised allure. There is nothing to be said about the cured fish Mrs Noren prepares, and which she serves with icy glasses of aquavit, save that if you have eaten it, then you can die happy.

Some folk can't tune in to this distinctive, singular Dunworley. They find the furnishings too stark, too simple; they find the tastes too unsubdued, too urgent. The acolytes, of course, like the Shaker plainness in the design, for it doesn't distract from the food, and the acolytes say that there is nowhere else like Dunworley and that the food is unforgettable. There is only one way, of course, to discover if you are acolyte, or unimpressed, and whatever conclusion you draw, a pilgrimage to Butlerstown is mighty fun.

● **OPEN:** Summer Lunch 1pm-3pm. Dinner from 6.30pm Wed-Sun. Closed Nov and Jan-early Mar.
● **AVERAGE PRICE:** Dinner £20. No Service Charge.
● **CREDIT CARDS:** Visa, Access/Master, Amex, Diners.

● **NOTES:** Restaurant Licence (plus bring your own wine for £2 corkage). Wheelchair Access. Children – highchairs, half portions. Recommended for Vegetarians. The restaurant is well signposted from Timoleague, and from Clonakilty.

GARNISH HOUSE
Hansi Lucey
Western Road, Cork
Co Cork
Tel: (021) 275111
Fax: (021) 273872

Hansi Lucey is a paragon of virtues, a woman who improvises on the theme of hospitality with the skill and judgement of a Heifetz.

Before she turned her hand to the business of bed and breakfasting, Mrs Lucey was a nursing sister, and it is this she associates as her gift in the people business, though such decent friendliness is something instinctive, not something that can be learned.

"How are ye? Did ye sleep well? Were ye comfortable? Would ye like some more hot toast – it's on its way. Lovely morning. How are ye?" On and on it goes, this wonderful litany of welcomes and solicitations, spontaneous, genuine, disarming, enveloping. Mrs Lucey wants you to be comfortable. She wants you to have a good time. And she and her staff will do all in their power to make sure you do have a good time, will do anything to ensure your comfort.

The rooms in Garnish House are naturally cosy and, of course, they contain all the bits and bobs and whatnots you might conceivably need, some even come with jacuzzis.

More than anything, however, it is the tenderness, a tenderness found in the lovely soft climb of those Cork accents – the way in which "You" is softened and abbreviated to the delightful "Ye" – which ye remember and which ye treasure. There are literally dozens of B&B's on this strip of the Western Road. But there is only one Hansi Lucey.

● **OPEN:** 365 days per year.
● **ROOMS:** 14 rooms, all en suite.
● **AVERAGE PRICE:**
£19-£26 per person sharing, £30 single.
No Service Charge.
● **CREDIT CARDS:**
Visa, Access/Master, Amex, Diners.

● **NOTES:**
No Restaurant facilities, but will offer light snacks if required.
No Licence.
No Wheelchair Access.
Children – high seats, cots, babysitting.
Recommended for Vegetarians.
Pets accommodated.
Enclosed car park.
The Western Road is the beginning of the road to Killarney, the N22, and adjacent to the centre of Cork.

HEIR ISLAND RESTAURANT ISLAND COTTAGE ⊗⊖
John Desmond & Ellmary Fenton
Roaringwater Bay, nr Skibbereen,
Co Cork
Tel: (028) 38102

If you wanted to do something unlikely, then how about this.

Open a small restaurant.

On an island.

The sort of island which means that your customers, having made their way down to the far reaches of West Cork in the first place, must, then, also make a boat journey across, in a small boat, in order to eat.

To complete this crazy idea, offer only one set menu each evening.
No choice, no matter who is dining.

John Desmond and Ellmary Fenton's Island Cottage, on Heir Island off the coast of West Cork, does all these things.

It represents something so magnificently unlikely and so defiantly unreal, that it was surely assured of success. Indeed, the inaccessibility of Heir Island has proven to be one of its greatest attractions.

For one thing, the boat journey across is so entrancing that you find yourself talking in Moon-in-June couplets even before you have hit the island: the sky, the sea, the instant comradeship with the other diners.
As for the food, there are important precedents for John Desmond's refusal to cook a multiple choice menu. Alice Waters in San

Francisco's famed Chez Panisse offers only one dinner menu each evening. In London, Sally Clarke does the same. The only important rule about restaurant cooking, ultimately, is that it should be good, and on this Mr Desmond scores handsomely.

Skill and tactility are bedfellows in his work, and dinner is a riot of lush flavours balanced with graceful tempering, so much so that, on one memorable visit here, the entire congregation of eaters broke into spontaneous applause when Mr Desmond shyly peeked his head out of the kitchen.

The food, the calm service, the camaraderie: it is not like anywhere else, or anything else, an evening on Heir Island.

● **OPEN:** Apr-Nov for bookings of six minimum (less will be accommodated if the restaurant has a booking).
Mon-Sun in season.
(Ask details of boat times).
● **AVERAGE PRICE:**
Dinner £18. No Service Charge.
Boatman charges approx. £3 per head.
● **CREDIT CARDS:** No Credit Cards.

● **NOTES:**
Wine Licence.
No Wheelchair Access.
Children – no facilities.
No Vegetarian menu.
The best boat to take leaves from Cunnamore. Driving from Skibbereen to Ballydehob, turn left at Church Cross (signposted to Heir Island). Keep going until the road ends at the Cunnamore car park. The boat trip is automatically booked when you book the restaurant.

THE IVORY TOWER RESTAURANT ◎⊖
Seamus O'Connell
The Exchange Buildings
35 Princes Street, Cork, Co Cork
Tel: (021) 274665

The two most important things that can be said about Seamus O'Connell's cooking are as follows.

Firstly, that he can do things other people couldn't manage to do in a month of Sundays. Furthermore, with the stuff they can do, he can usually do it better.

Secondly, he is a chef who is unafraid of failure: he aims for the stars, every time. When he hits them, then you know just what a supercharged cook with a driving ambition can achieve. When he doesn't hit them, then his food is all-fall-down. With someone else, this might be annoying. With Mr O'Connell, it is part of his glory, the agony which attends the ecstasy of The Ivory Tower.

He is a virtuoso, with all the excitements which that description entails. And these excitements can be intense, with menus that are utterly thrilling just to look at, never mind to actually eat. But when you do eat them, then, wow! A sublime gratin of asparagus and sweetbreads. An amazing pizza of duck and aubergine, with a yeasted bread dough base. A confit of duck served with a venison sausage and a pear and elderflower sauce. Perfect eel boudin on red cabbage with a sorrel sauce. This is outrageously inventive food, outrageously personal, and unconcerned with commercial niceties.

"One cannot help but admire these two: their coltish beauty is coupled with a touching, low-key sense of dignity", was how the food writer Emily Green described Mr O'Connell and his cousin, Clare O'Connor, with whom he shares the running of The Ivory Tower.

"His eccentricity is much more than shirt-deep", continued Ms Green. "While he has the gentle, slightly distracted quality of a jazzman, Mr O'Connell is a heat-and-sizzle chef, and a remarkably good one".

Like any good jazzman, Mr O'Connell also has remarkably good taste in music, which means that not only the pots and pans rattle and roll in The 'Tower: the sounds are ultra-cool, and so is this inspiring space. The only trouble lies in deciding which jazzman Mr O'Connell's style puts you in mind of. Unique? Unpredictable? Uncommercial? As of now, our vote goes to Eric Dolphy.

● **OPEN:** Noon-4pm, 6.30pm-11pm Tue-Sun.
● **AVERAGE PRICE:** Lunch under £10. Dinner £15-£20. No Service Charge.
● **CREDIT CARDS:** Visa, Access/Master.

● **NOTES:** Wine Licence. No Wheelchair Access. Children – high chair. Recommended for Vegetarians. Upstairs, on the corner of Princes Street and Plunkett Street, just off Patrick's Street. Look for the first floor sign.

LETTERCOLLUM HOUSE ⊗⊗⊖
Con McLoughlin & Karen Austen
Timoleague, Co Cork
Tel: (023) 46251

"God, it's gorgeous!"

When your lunch companion utters something as effusive as this, you tend to pay attention. When they are as effusive as this, having gone no further into lunch than to break off and bite into a single piece of bread, then it is time to pay serious attention.

So, if you are having lunch or dinner in Lettercollum House, just outside the village of Timoleague, then make sure you start at the very beginning.

Break off and bite into a piece of bread and, as the rush of yeasty liveliness assails your taste buds and the great span of flavour just goes on and on, try to see if you can resist such exclamations of delight. You won't get very far, believe us.

Not, at least, if the first course is a sublime seafood sausage with a note-perfect chive butter, or a mussel and pumpkin soup accented with a dash of pesto.

By the time you get to main courses, you are likely to be calling on the heavenly choirs for assistance to describe the total deliciousness of Con McLoughlin's cooking: a tarragon roast chicken so perfectly rendered that it could be the basis for a Masterclass on roasting; gorgeously creamy spanokopitta, the amazement of a plate of vegetables which have dawdled in from the walled garden and been transformed into a festival of fresh tastes.

Food this simple and pure is always a treat, no matter how often you eat it, and perfect desserts like lemon tart or floating islands with home-made vanilla ice-cream merely cap the innocent joy which is at the heart of eating at this funky, splendid place.

If you are five or fifty, rich or poor, frail or sound in limb and wind, Lettercollum promises delight for all.

All in all, this is a demon, darling place, right from the democratic air of dinner, with backpackers seated at tables next to folk who arrive in limos, right from the tender spirit of young and old conjoined at Sunday lunchtimes, right the way through to your own romantic dinner, with the kids parked happily upstairs, sound asleep.

Do note, also, that Lettercollum also feature cookery classes during the winter, which Karen Austin oversees, and they can also play host to small conferences.

● **OPEN:** 7.30pm-9.30pm Tue-Sun, 1.30pm-3.30pm Sun
(Check times out of season).
● **AVERAGE PRICE:** Lunch £10.
Dinner £13.50-£18.50.
● **CREDIT CARDS:**
Visa, Access/Mastercard, Diners.

● **NOTES:**
No Service Charge.
Wine Licence.
Wheelchair Access.
Children – high chairs and half portions.
Recommended for Vegetarians.
Just outside Timoleague, driving west, and clearly signposted.

LISS ARD LAKE LODGE ®Ⓐ
Claudia Meister
Skibbereen, Co Cork
Tel: (028) 22365

In the glorious Liss Ard Lodge, you will find some of the most singular, singularly impressive cooking in Ireland.

Claudia Meister's recipes do not use animal fats in their preparation, a bold move which forces both the chef and her assistant, Fred, into a free-fall of creativity with every single dish. What is most impressive, aside from the solid seizure of flavour which the food exhibits so boldly, is the fact that the cooking is not an abstract exercise, some sort of theme stolen from the likes of Michel Guerard. It is powerful, absorbing food, beautifully orchestrated and achieved.

Ms Meister achieves her ambition of cooking in a style which allows one to contemplate the beauty of the preparation – that startling sea-vegetable sculpting which is the leek and pine kernel cannelloni; an amazing pavé of chocolate which might have been designed by the extraordinary Japanese costume designer Eiko Ishioka, so flirty and precocious does it look on the plate – but which never masks the beauty of the flavours which the food contains. This cooking is intricate and feminine: sea scallops with a sauce vierge are evanescent; a beef consommé with foie gras parcels is as evocative an expression of unadorned beauty as is the Lodge itself.

Creativity and originality runs

rampant through the six courses of dinner: a pithivier of vegetables comes in a pin-cushion pastry; little tortellinis line up like bishops' hats atop a chessboard of pulses and tapenade; a pill-box of potato accompanies a perfectly rendered roast partridge; a hot calvados soufflé is shaped like a cossack hat.

And you do not, at the end of dinner, feel that you have missed anything, or that something has been lacking. The tastes are so direct, the preparations so exquisite, the choreography of dinner so expertly conceived and executed, that you are lost in admiration. Ms Meister's food points a way forward for Irish cooking, away from the dead-hand of emulsions, the shout of butter, the cloud of cream. Anyone who wants a taste of the future – a gorgeous taste of the future – will get to Liss Ard as soon as possible.

● **OPEN:** All year.
Dinner 7pm-10.30pm Mon-Sun.
(Booking essential).
● **ROOMS:** Ten rooms, all en suite.
● **AVERAGE PRICE:**
B&B £110-£130 per person sharing.
Dinner £29.
No Service Charge.
● **CREDIT CARDS:**
Visa, Access/Master, Amex, Diners.

● **NOTES:**
Full Licence.
Wheelchair Access.
Children – high chair.
Recommended for Vegetarians.
Leave Skibbereen on the Tragumna road, the house is signposted, and their tower gates – a folly – are very distinctive.

LONGUEVILLE HOUSE ❀❀❀✪
William, Jane & Aisling O'Callaghan
Mallow
Co Cork
Tel: (022) 47156, Fax: (022) 47459

William O'Callaghan is an outrageously talented cook, a chef whose quiet concentration is counterpointed by a culinary imagination which seems to know no boundary. He is outrageously inventive, and marries together a virtuoso technique with a love of flavour appropriate to the countryman he is.

Added to this brilliance is a total, intense commitment to cooking: Mr O'Callaghan gets into it, he gets involved. This involvement means that, with each dish, he is on the hunt for the true, inherent flavours of the food. In the case of Longueville House, this has particular resonance. For the house is almost self-sufficient and, here, one eats the food of the house, in the house, cooked by the young chef of the house. The local food, the local house, the local boy: it is a mesmerising trio. Famous food critics have, in private moments, let it be known that they have never eaten finer food anywhere.

Whatever one chooses to eat is marked by pyrotechnical excellence – Longueville lamb fillets and baby courgettes set in a tomato concassé are gravity-defying; a ravioli of prawns with their juices scented with basil are secretive, hidden – and drop-dead deliciousness. William O'Callaghan's fluency extends right from the simplest fried fish – fillets of black sole with a gâteau of garden vegetables – to a crisp appreciation of fowl and game cookery – breast of farmyard duck with a ginger and coriander sauce accompanied by a potato straw cake, is something to die for. Desserts are stunningly fine: a clafoutis of garden plums with almond iced crystal; a mille feuille of wild blackberries.

Whilst eating in Longueville is a sublime indulgence, it is also a remarkably balanced one, and the courses follow seamlessly, with nothing discordant allowed to interrupt the procession of fine food. The entire experience is quite organic: complete of and unto itself. Service is, of course, excellent: busy, effective, quietly boisterous. The wine list, and do note that William's father produces a small amount of white wine each year on the estate, is superb.

● **OPEN:** Mar-late Dec.
Restaurant open to non residents
Sun lunch and dinner, if pre booked.
● **ROOMS:** Thirteen rooms, all en suite.
Seven suites.
● **AVERAGE PRICE:**
B&B £58-£80 per person sharing.
Sun lunch £17, dinner £27-£28.
No Service Charge.
● **CREDIT CARDS:**
Visa, Access/Master, Amex.

● **NOTES:**
Full Licence.
Wheelchair Access.
Children – high chair.
Recommended for Vegetarians.
3 miles west of Mallow on the N72 to Killarney, at the big crossroads.

THE OYSTERCATCHER RESTAURANT ⊛ ✪
Sylvia & Bill Patterson
Oysterhaven, Co Cork
Tel: (021) 770822

Bill Patterson calls his starter dishes "The Seducers" – Hot Smoked Ummera Salmon on Blinis with a Leek Sauce; Oyster Sausage on a Saffron Sauce; Bresoala with Sundried Tomatoes and Fresh Parmesan, Grilled Inagh Goat's Cheese with Grape and Pinenut Salad; Local Oysters baked with Almonds, Garlic and Parsley.

They arrive at the table, and you begin. Voices die down, golden silence reigns. You have just been seduced.

When they are finished, responses are, usually, something like this: "The problem with this is trying to stretch it out, to make it last as long as possible", or: "I don't want to eat this, I just want to make it last".

But eat it you must. Bill Patterson's food is irresistible, as tasty as anything cooked by anyone in this country. Built on a bedrock of peerless ingredients, he works his magic, a magic that can strike one dumb.

It's not just the food in The Oystercatcher which weaves a spell, however. The restaurant itself is a picture-postcard cottage, at the cross of the road in Oysterhaven, five miles out of Kinsale and not much further from Cork city itself. Winking red lights line the eaves, and inside the room is a romantic, understated space. The glasses on the table are tall and sparkling, and one enjoys a cool sense of relaxation alongside the tingling note of expectation which a cook like Bill Patterson engenders.

Main courses merely increase the magic: Marinated Tuna Steak with Roma Tomato and Caper Sauce; King Prawns on a Garlic and Ginger Sauce with Oyster Juice; a mildly curried Breast of Chicken with a waggish poppadum on top; a Lobster Charlotte with a Basil Scented Sauce; a Tournedo topped with goat's cheese.

Desserts, like crème brûlée or a fresh fruit pavlova, are delicate and modest, another signature of Mr Patterson's work, for the rhythm of a dinner in The Oystercatcher starts with a bang but then works gradually towards simpler, lighter flavours. At the end, you have been seduced by beauty. And you want it to happen all over again.

● **OPEN:** 7.30pm-9.30pm Mon-Sat.
Closed Xmas, Easter mid Jan-mid Feb (low season bookings absolutely essential).
● **AVERAGE PRICE:** Dinner £24.95.
No Service Charge, except parties of six or more, 10%.
● **CREDIT CARDS:**
Visa, Access/Master, Amex.

● **NOTES:**
Wine Licence.
Wheelchair Access.
Children – every effort made to accommodate them.
Recommended for Vegetarians if given 24 hrs notice.
Follow signs for Oysterhaven, and the restaurant is just on your left before you go over the bridge into the village.

SCILLY HOUSE INN ▲
Karin Young & Bill Skelly
Scilly, Kinsale, Co Cork
Tel & Fax: (021) 772413

If one has a mind to build a luxury B&B, it is easy to simply chuck money in the direction of your idea and to hope that a shower of cash will buy you the sort of good taste which discriminating guests will seek out.

Easy, yes, but almost certainly doomed to failure, as certain large houses which have been built as B&Bs in Kinsale amply attest to. To create a luxury B&B you need, firstly, a sense of the place and importance of beauty, and the ability to make this beauty both tactile and, vitally, accessible. Karin Young's Scilly House, just out of Kinsale on the Scilly side, and perched on the hill peering across the harbour, is a place that solves the problem of accessible good taste and an envelopment of beauty, seemingly effortlessly.

The rooms are vast, and vastly comfortable, but never overstated: the colours in the traditional quilts and the furnishings play with light and space and easily accommodate the rafts of bright light which come hurling through the windows, bouncing back from the sea. One room is actually in a cottage set fast by the house. Downstairs there is, again, subtlety and understatement, things left to speak for themselves.

The understatement, it must be said, meets its Waterloo when it comes to the baths, which are gargantuan and, it appears from even the briefest skiffle through the rather fruity visitors' book, irresistible to one and all, all together. Whether you arrive with wishes of water-borne romance, either on the sea in some tub or, literally, in a Scilly House tub, or whether you prefer to keep your feet firmly on the ground, this is a romantic house, its attractions always evident, but always understated. The cooking is excellent and whilst prices are high, it is worth it.

● **OPENS:** Mid Apr-Oct.
● **ROOMS:** Six rooms and one separate cottage, all en suite.
● **AVERAGE PRICE:**
From £40 per person sharing, £65 single.
No Service Charge.
● **CREDIT CARDS:**
Visa, Access/Master, Amex.

● **NOTES:**
No restaurant facilities, plenty locally.
Wine Licence.
No Wheelchair Access.
Children – over twelve only.
No pets.
Scilly House is just outside the centre of Kinsale, around the corner from the Man Friday Restaurant, opposite the Spaniard pub.

SEVEN NORTH MALL ◬➔
Angela Hegarty
7 North Mall, Cork
Co Cork
Tel: (021) 397191

Whilst this handsome town house, down towards the end of the river malls in Cork city, has the standard requisites for the business traveller – the 'phone, the TV, the trouser press, the hairdrier, the luggage horse – it is no bland, anodyne shack-up for suits. Seven North Mall is valuable because of the cool, understated air it possesses, something which makes it operate – almost – as a retreat in the bubbling, busy city of Cork.

The air of understatement is seen in the appreciation of the importance of carefully chosen furnishings, carefully chosen utensils, carefully chosen addendums. Breakfast, thus, is a chance to peruse the papers which are left out, though the expertise of properly scrambled eggs is likely to demand your attention more stringently than any amount of news or gossip. Good coffee from a cafetiére, real orange juice and the gritty, warming tactility of Stephen Pearce crockery makes the meal truer, deeper.

There are chairs to lounge in, baths to submerge in and a pleasing attention in the housekeeping. The blankness and dull functionalism which annihilates any sense of comfort in the modern hotel where business folk might normally stay is absent here, and the tired worker can relax in a genuine, real environment, whilst the traveller is likely to revel in it.

The location of the house means that everywhere in the city is proximate, and walkable, especially some of Cork's best restaurants. For anyone arriving on the ferry at Cork it offers secure parking and an excellent first-night, last-night location.

- **OPEN:** All year except Xmas.
- **ROOMS:** Five rooms, all en suite.
- **AVERAGE PRICE:** £30 per person sharing. No Service Charge.
- **CREDIT CARDS:** Visa, Access/Master.

- **NOTES:**
No evening meals.
No Licence.
Wheelchair Access.
Pets (by arrangement).
Locked Car Park.
In Cork, keep driving down the northern quays. North Mall is after Pope's Quay.

TRAVARA LODGE ⒶⓇ
Mandy Guy
Courtmacsherry, Co Cork
Tel: (023) 46493

"With advance notice we do our best to accommodate any requests, i.e. ground floor room, cots, baby sitters, sea view, dogs, vegetarian meals, packed lunch, early breakfast etc", says Mandy Guy in this manifesto-like statement, and she means it.

Travara Lodge sits looking out onto the sea in the beautiful, pastel-painted village of Courtmacsherry, and Ms Guy works hard, extra hard, to make a success of both the little restaurant downstairs and the rooms upstairs. The desire to please, and the desire to help you have the very best time, is what motivates Ms Guy, and powers the hospitality of Travara Lodge.

The food she prepares in the evenings is simple, inviting, – john dory with a tomato and herb sauce; an old nugget like chicken Cordon

Bleu brought to life; sirloin steak with garlic butter – and it's always fine value, as is the short but quaffable selection of wines she culls from Galvin's in Cork. The rooms have pummelling showers and comfortable beds, and those at the front of the house have super views across the calm inlet with its baby-blue water and baby-blue sky. These are the rooms to chase after.

Don't worry, by the way, should you fear that Courtmacsherry might prove to be as twee in spirit as one might imagine from its slightly kiddy-book appearance. The loveliness of the village conceals a more-than-slightly-wild streak amidst the locals. Turn up for the Courtmacsherry Shrimp Festival in September, when the Hilarious Shrimp Cookery Competition slugs it out with a Shrimp Spitting Competition (how do you teach a shrimp to spit?) and when local cooks and producers combine to present their wares, and you will see the place at its quirkily crazy best.

- **OPEN:** Mar-Oct.
- **ROOMS:** Seven rooms, all en suite.
- **AVERAGE PRICE:** £18.50 per person sharing, No Service Charge – 10% discount for 1 week's booking. Dinner £15.
- **CREDIT CARDS:** Visa, Access/Master.

- **NOTES:**
Wine Licence.
Wheelchair Access – one en suite ground floor room.
Children – high chairs, cots, babysitting.
Vegetarian meals a Monday speciality
Pets accommodated on special request.
Centre of Courtmacsherry.

BEGINISH RESTAURANT ®
John & Pat Moore
Green Street, Dingle
Co Kerry
Tel: (066) 51588

Pat Moore is a serious cook, and a seriously skillful one. She has already created one of the most talked-about dishes in recent years in Ireland – a hot rhubarb soufflé tart of such ethereal tenderness and drop-dead deliciousness that it hits the senses with the shock of waking from a dream – but there is much more to her skills than those of the talented patissier.

Her cooking reveals a cook who is hungrily inquisitive, her work full of those little gestures which announce the improvisations and experiment-ations of a cook who wants to learn more and more. One of the greatest errors made by many chefs is their disinterest in the work of their peers. Mrs Moore has not only eaten the food of the great chefs, she is a perceptive critic of the work of even the most luminary individuals, and she knows how to assimilate the strengths of other people's work into her cooking, and how to avoid their shortcomings.

Where this comes most happily into play is in her appreciation for flavour, and the need to locate and capture the integral flavour of an ingredient whilst, at the same moment, contrasting or comforting it with an apposite sauce.

With flaky, sweet crab meat, she will combine the shellfish with a chive mayonnaise, whilst tender pinky prawns will have a sharply spiced mayonnaise to play against.

A fillet of turbot will sit on a scrumptious bed of potato purée with a clean chive sauce circling the dish, whilst roasted john dory will have a dazzlingly colourful brunoise of vegetables tapestried around the dish with a creamy mustard sauce perfectly accenting the freshness and liveliness of the fish.

Tastes are very positive and happy, and the sense of balance in the main courses is instinctively judged. There are, of course, the essential nods to Saturday night specials – beef fillet with rostis, spring lamb, Beginish lobster – but fish rightly pre-dominates on the menu: black sole on the bone meuniere; fillet of brill garnished with a julienne of leek. When in Dingle, you want to be in the Beginish. Simple as that.

● **OPEN:** Mid Mar-mid Nov.
12.30pm-2.15pm, 6pm-10pm Tue-Sun.
● **AVERAGE PRICE:** Lunch £2.50-£10,
Dinner £20.
No Service Charge.
● **CREDIT CARDS:**
Visa, Access/Master, Diners.

● **NOTES:**
Full Pub Licence.
No Wheelchair Access.
Children – welcome.
Note: Pat Moore also operates a number of self-catering apartments. All of them very well equipped, comfortable and furnished with typical good taste. Best of all, they are only a stone's throw from the restaurant.
Almost opposite the Catholic church, half way up Green Street at the top of the town.

D'ARCY'S ⊕⊕
Matthew & Aileen d'Arcy
Main Street, Kenmare, Co Kerry
Tel & Fax: (064) 41589

Matt d'Arcy's Old Bank House may be set in somewhat simpler premises than the grandeur of The Park Hotel, his old stomping ground just down the hill in Kenmare where he was head chef for many years, but the rich complexity and lavish culinary control of d'Arcy's cooking are every bit as evident here as before.

"Flawless technique and under-stated flavours", were the essentials of his style, The New York Times said some years back. More accurately, they said "Some of Mr d'Arcy's combinations are daring". Indeed they are.

His love of variation and complication, of finding new alliances, is rampant throughout an agonising-to-choose-from menu: warm ravioli of prawn mousse with a sweet pepper scented butter; salmon with noodles in a light curry sauce; chicken and noodle soup with star anise; scallops fried in the pan with leeks and grapes. All of this is unexpected, original for an Irish chef, and it makes Mr d'Arcy's dishes endlessly fascinating.

At the same time as one relishes the inventiveness and unexpect-edness, you are also struck by the fact that this cooking, with its impressive architecture of design and concentrated focus of taste, manages to be both classic and, at the same time, very modern. Such intelligent striding across the barriers of taste

and the styles of time demands a singular discipline. Matt d'Arcy has it.

The dining room is a simple, enjoyable space, perhaps at its best on cool evenings when the fire burns bright, and there is a good bottle of wine to enjoy with this good food. The staff on the floor share Mr d'Arcy's confidence.

- **OPEN:** 6pm-11pm Mon-Sun (Apr-Oct), 7pm-10.30pm Fri-Sun (Oct-Mar).
- **ROOMS:** Five rooms, two en suite, three share one bathroom.
- **AVERAGE PRICE:**
B&B £16 per person sharing.
Dinner £17.50. No Service Charge.
- **CREDIT CARDS:** Visa, Access/Master.

- **OPEN:**
Wine Licence.
Wheelchair Access.
Children – welcome, half portions.
Vegetarian meals only with prior notice
At the top end of Main Street, on the left hand side as you drive up the hill.

LOAVES AND FISHES ⊛⊖
Helen Mullane & Armel Whyte
Caherdaniel
Co Kerry
Tel: (0667) 5273

Loaves and Fishes is a miraculously good restaurant. Why? Because it is enchanting, simple as that. You turn off the Ring of Kerry at Caherdaniel, head a little bit down the hill in the direction of the sea, walk in the door, and the spell of Loaves and Fishes will seize you instantly. It is a place of rapture.

Helen Mullane and Armel Whyte originate and orchestrate this enchantment. Her skills at front of house are a model of how to do the job: poised, confident, astute, caring, no one does it better.

His skills in the kitchen produce exactly the sort of food to suit the rooms. Friendly, flavour-addicted and fun, Mr Whyte is attuned to the riches which surround his restaurant. In season they will both be down on the foreshore collecting salty green samphire and other wild plants and leaves. The combination of Mr Whyte's subtle, classical style and the ruddiness of the wild flavours he likes to work with, makes for a synthesis which is mesmerising

But the great achievement of this duo is to create the sort of space, and the sort of food, which can be both homey and stylish, carefree and rigorous, the yin and yang of eating and enjoyment.

● **OPEN:** Easter-Sept.
7pm-9.30pm Tue-Sun.
● **AVERAGE PRICE:**
Dinner £18-£24. No Service Charge.
● **CREDIT CARDS:**
Visa, Access/Master.

● **NOTES:**
Wine Licence.
Wheelchair Access (but not to toilet).
Children – no facilities.
Caherdaniel is on the Ring of Kerry, about 45 mins from Kenmare, 10 mins from Waterville. Loaves & Fishes is signposted from the main road.

PACKIE'S ⊗ ⊖
Maura Foley
Henry Street, Kenmare, Co Kerry
Tel: (064) 41508

Maura Foley is one of the finest cooks in Ireland, possibly the greatest fish cook in the country, and amongst the least known cooks in the country.

Folk remember great dinners eaten in The Lime Tree, in Kenmare, when Mrs Foley owned it. They will recall a black sole which achieved perfection, and the respect shown to simple things such as a purée of turnips, or vanilla ice cream.

But most likely they will not think of Mrs Foley as the cook.

They may remember fish cookery of utter mellifluousness eaten in the charming, youthful embrace of Packie's restaurant – cod baked with a cheese bechamel, or the same fish en papilotte – but again it will be the memory of a splendid evening, rather than the knowledge of just who cooked the dish, which remains.

For thirty years, Maura Foley has cooked wonderful food, and cooked it with the skill and love of the patient, modest woman she is.

Her food is incredibly delicious – above all else this is her gift – and she has been happy to stay in the kitchen making this food, for all these years.

Her devotion to her kitchen, to her restaurants, to her standards, has made her the grand-mère of Irish cooking.

She has defined a style of cooking which, in its lack of artifice, in its integrity, seems quintessentially Irish.

The Irishness extends also to unpretentious and friendly service, which brings this small room to life every night of the season. But, if people perhaps don't figure Mrs Foley as the woman behind all of this delicious food, what they will never forget is the delight of the experience. The dignity in her work and the dignity in her cooking conjoin, here, to make Packie's one of the best restaurants in Ireland.

- ● **OPEN:** End Feb-end Dec.
5.30pm-10pm Mon-Sat.
- ● **AVERAGE PRICE:**
Dinner £15.
No Service Charge.
- ● **CREDIT CARDS:** Visa, Access/Master.

- ● **NOTES:**
Wine Licence.
Wheelchair Access (through side door).
Children – high chairs.
Recommended for Vegetarians.
In the centre of Kenmare.

THE PARK HOTEL ®Ⓐ
Francis Brennan
Kenmare, Co Kerry
Tel: (064) 41200

If they wished to crown a king in the kingdom of Kerry, they could only choose one man. Francis Brennan, the hotelier's hotelier, is the magician of hospitality. No one does it better in Ireland, and we would happily take bets that no one does it better anywhere. He is consummate, in a class of his own.

The Park Hotel is his own kingdom, and he works it with the benevolent control of a kindly monarch. No detail is too small for Mr Brennan to attend to, and he leads by example rather than command. To see him at work is to be inspired, to want to be able to do what he does.

But you can't do what he does, and no one can. True, he has some of the finest staff imaginable working with him – Jim McCarthy and Tony Daly, to name but two, are maestros of their professions – but The Park is, all told, all about Mr Brennan.

Bruno Schmidt directs the kitchen, and his cooking perfectly understands and answers the hotel's need for disciplined sumptuousness. Quenelles of foie gras with grilled black pudding; loin of veal on a bed of goat's cheese; cassoulet of poussin and kohl-rabi with asparagus; poached fillet of beef in a lemon grass bouillon, chocolate cups filled with passion fruit mousse. The wine list is fabulous, service is immaculate, and The Park Hotel is an unforgettable experience.

- ● **OPEN:** Easter-Nov & Xmas. Dinner to non residents 7pm-8.45pm Mon-Sun.
- ● **AVERAGE PRICE:** B&B £96-£115 low season, £115-£138 high season.
Dinner £38.
No Service Charge.
- ● **CREDIT CARDS:**
Visa, Access/Master, Amex, Diners.

- ● **NOTES:**
Full Pub Licence.
Wheelchair Access.
Children – welcome, cots, high chairs.
At the top of the hill in Kenmare.

THE MUSTARD SEED AT ECHO LODGE ◈◈◈ ⊕
Dan Mullane
Ballingarry
Co Limerick
Tel: (069) 68508

It is a mark of the ambitions which Dan Mullane holds for Echo Lodge that, following a decade of running one of the most successful restaurants in the country, he should change tack and embark on the costly, elaborate adventure that is Echo Lodge.

"It's not a brash country house that looks as if its been planted here", he says. "It looks like it's been here forever". Seven acres surround the house, a fine Victorian edifice, but what counts, in truth, is the presence of Mr Mullane.

He is one of the most consummate and capable of Irish restaurateurs, a quiet innovator, an adept at the business of placing people at their ease and knowing how to help them to have a good time.

For Mr Mullane is a romantic soul, and loves the meeting and greeting, the sharing and caring of the hospitality business, and his grasp of the necessary skills of the restaurateur is absolute.

If he has the knack, he also has the right sort of good taste for a house like this. Restraint and a flamboyant understatement are his style, both in design and food.

With chef David Norris, the cooking in the new Mustard Seed promises more of the old Mustard Seed.

That is to say, we can expect the continuation and development of a style of cooking that plays games with the disciplines of the classics: grilled goat's cheese with a roasted beetroot dressing; pork terrine glazed with an apple and clove jelly; steamed escalope of salmon with a quenelle of pasta and a lemon and chive beurre blanc; quenelles of pork fillet with a fennel seed crust; sirloin of beef with an onion and garlic cream.

More than a decade ago, when he opened the Mustard Seed, Dan Mullane created an oasis of style and reality in Adare. He himself, tellingly, describes Echo Lodge as "an oasis of good living in the heart of the Golden Vale".

He likes oases. So will you.

● **OPEN:** Mid Mar-mid Jan.
Dinner for non residents 7pm-9.30pm Mon-Sat.
House Dinner Party 8pm Sun.
(Residents only).
● **ROOMS:**
Ten rooms, all en suite, one suite.
● **AVERAGE PRICE:**
B&B £50-£60 low season;
£60-£75 high season.
Dinner £26-£28. No Service Charge.
● **CREDIT CARDS:**
Visa, Access/Master, Amex.

● **NOTES:**
Wine Licence.
Children – welcome.
No Wheelchair Access.
From Adare take the N21 Killarney road for 1 mile. Turn left and follow signs for Ballingarry. In Ballingarry take the Newcastle West road for 500 yards where you will see the entrance on your right.

BALLYTEIGUE HOUSE ◎
Margaret & Dick Johnson
Bruree
nr Charleville
Co Limerick
Tel: (063) 90575

We live in times when enthusiasm and unbridled expressiveness are increasingly rare.

So, to counter this drought of deliriously enunciated and giddily expressed happiness, let us quote from a letter sent to us by a happy visitor who stayed in Ballyteigue House, Margaret Johnson's fine place, for no less than ten days:

"The service was impeccable and the personal touch of our welcoming hostess was never missing. It was such a surprise to know that she even cooked all the meals herself and what meals!!"

Not just one, note that, but two exclamation marks. When was the last time you came across a pair of exclamation marks in a letter?

Most likely, you were seven years old and were writing that dreaded return-to-school essay: "What I did on my holidays".

Well, no matter what you are doing on your holidays, you will be hard pressed to find a better place to stay.

A high, wide, handsome house which is achingly comfortable and astonishingly inexpensive, this is a place in which to do nothing very much whatsoever – flop in front of the fire with a mind-emptying mag, nap away the afternoon, focus on dinner for an hour beforehand dreaming of what magic Margaret is

cooking up – or you could shoot and fish and do other estimable sporty fixations should that be to your taste.

Margaret Johnson makes it rather difficult to drag yourself away from the house however.

She is a terrifically sociable woman who makes you feel welcome in about thirty seconds flat. And the warmth of the welcome works whether you are jet-jaundiced or road-weary – and do note that the location of the house makes it a great stop for first and last nights if you are using Shannon airport – or bright-eyed and holiday-moded-and rarin' to go.

Whatever your motivations Ballyteigue, with its relaxed quirkiness and unpretentious ease, is somewhere splendid.

● **OPEN:** All year except Xmas.
● **ROOMS:** 5 rooms, 4 en suite, single with private bathroom.
● **AVERAGE PRICE:**
£18 per person. Dinner, £16.
No Service Charge.
● **CREDIT CARDS:**
Visa, Access/Master.

● **NOTES:**
Dinner for residents only, book by noon.
No Licence (bring your own wine).
No Wheelchair Access.
Children – 50% reduction if sharing.
Pets by arrangement only (not in bedrooms).
1 hour from Shannon airport.
Going towards Charleville, heading south on the main Cork road, look out for the Jet Petrol Station. Ballyteigue is signposted from the next turn right.

BALLYCORMAC HOUSE ⚠

Herb & Christine Quigley
Aglish, Borrisokane, Co Tipperary
Tel: (067) 21129
Fax: (067) 21200

Some cooking is so urgently good that it brings out the Samaritan in us.

About half-way through the bowl of sorrel soup, which started a dinner in Ballycormac House, a soup so good it was effectively a text-book study in soup-making, we actually wished we had a mobile telephone on hand, just so we could start calling our friends and tell them to get themselves down to Ballycormac, quick.

This sort of thing doesn't happen too often, and rarely in a country house.

For the most part, country house cooking in Ireland is generous, adequate, appropriate to the place.

But it doesn't knock your socks off.

The dinner prepared by Herb and Christine Quigley in Ballycormac House had us screaming with delight.

Not only did it offer the sort of definitively rendered tastes you hope to find – a perfectly roasted rack of lamb, a fabulous tart of carrot and Swiss chard – it also offered a mashed potato and goat's cheese gratin, where the potatoes had first been cooked with cloves of garlic, then puréed and mixed with grated goat's cheese, chopped scallions beaten in to the mix, and then the dish was browned in a hot oven. It was amazing, and we just could not stop eating it.

Such fine cooking would satisfy any clamorous appetite, but there is such an element of surprise to Herb and Christine's cooking that you find yourself lying in bed wondering what little twists and revisions they will have worked on breakfast, what bread will have been baked to start the day.

You are not disappointed.

The homemade sausage with some scrambled eggs is perfectly flavoured with apple and sage, and the extra element of lemon zest keeps the flavour fresh.

With still-hot griddle scones baked that morning, and just-right fig and gooseberry preserves, some warm stewed apple and sharp yogurt, it is a breakfast to remember.

Herb and Christine Quigley are cooks who are endlessly excited by cooking. Their excitement is utterly contagious.

● **OPEN:** All year except Xmas.
● **ROOMS:** Five rooms, all en suite.
● **AVERAGE PRICE:**
B&B £30 per person sharing.
Dinner £23. No Service Charge.
● **CREDIT CARDS:**
Visa, Access/Master, Eurocard

● **NOTES:**
Full Licence.
No Wheelchair Access.
Children – cots, babysitting.
No Pets in house.
Take the Portumna Road out of Borrisokane, for half a mile then take the first turn right. Keep going to the end of this road (about three miles) and then follow the signs for the house.

CHEZ HANS ®

Hans Peter & Jason Matthias
Cashel, Co Tipperary
Tel: (062) 61177

"Thank you, Lord, for preserving me to eat another dinner at Chez Hans", intones the jowly, prelate-perfect man who had, clearly, strolled out of the pages of G.K. Chesterton.

He speaks for us all.

With the image of the Last Supper staring down at you, with its poignant bitterness, the fact that Chez Hans was formerly a church makes it the perfect place to break bread, especially in the company of prelate-perfect types.

Its secret lies with its magical ability, despite twenty-five years of business, to make every evening seem like a first night.

The staff are sweet and keen and professional, and only the music leaves anything to be desired: with that vaulting roof and the sun-comprehending glass, you tend to want to hear Bach cantatas, so getting some dithery diddledy-eye is disappointing.

Jason Matthias' food, however, does not fail to hit the spot. It is punchy and sustaining, almost old-fashioned. A red pepper and roasted artichoke soup is direct and powerful in flavour, perfect with the superb pumpernickle bread they serve.

Quail with wild mushrooms will be perfectly roasted and will have achieved that glorious, irresistible richness which forces you to eat the birds with your fingers.

This is unapologetically sumptuous food.

Vegetables in Chez Hans are, it seems, prepared for someone who is girding themselves to gather winter wheat by hand: mounds of spicy champ, a lather of crisp carrots, lots and lots of broccoli, a drumlin of creamy mushrooms.

They don't gather the winter wheat by hand in Tipperary anymore but, clearly, no one has told them that in Chez Hans.

A perfect Cointreau-flavoured soufflé with a kiwi sauce will counterpoint all this indulgence with its effete precision.

And, then, like all the happy families and couples and clerics, with their well-fed smiles and their contented relaxation, you will mutter, "Thank you, Lord, for preserving me to eat another dinner at Chez Hans".

The prelate-perfect man out of the pages of G.K. Chesterton said it. Everyone thinks it.

● **OPEN:** 6.30pm-9.30pm Tue-Sat.
(Closed last 3 weeks in Jan).
● **AVERAGE PRICE:** Dinner £25.
No Service Charge.
● **CREDIT CARDS:**
Visa, Access/Master.

● **NOTES:**
Full Licence.
Wheelchair Access.
Children – no facilities.
Just beside the Rock of Cashel, and clearly signposted from the Dublin-Cork road as you come into Cashel going south.

INCH HOUSE ⊛⊕
The Egan Family
Thurles
Co Tipperary
Tel: (0504) 51348

In mid-August, you can purr down the long driveway up to Inch House, through a field of ripening winter wheat which waves and whistles golden and graceful right up to the edge of the driveway, and the effect is as magical as a van Gogh landscape, but with you secreted in the midst of it.

It is enchanting, and almost unique, for there are few occasions where Irish farmers grow their crops without a boundary and right up to the road's edge.

The enchantment continues in Inch House itself.

It is a fine slab of a place, with a snaking stairway that almost calls for you to clamber up it the second you walk through the door, and a drawing room straight out of that mystical child's imagination which spells William Morris.

The breakfast room, which is transformed in the evening into a dining room where Ailish Maher works her magic, is tall and aristocratic, washed with the soft morning light of Tipperary, and the perfect location for enjoying breakfast.

That you will enjoy breakfast is undoubted, not just for the fine compotes – the strawberry and rhubarb is a beaut – and the freshly baked breads, but also for the quiet care of Mrs Egan.

Some folk don't believe in making things easy for themselves, and the Egans are amongst that hardy troupe. Not content with a squad of children – eight in all, count 'em – and a farm, they run Inch House efficiently and effectively for guests, and for dinner diners.

Ms Maher's food is both ambitious and consoling: hot and sour prawns; peach and tomato soup; rack of lamb with a parsnip purée; breast of duck with a caramelised onion sauce; a cheeseboard of the glorious Tipperary cheeses.

All in all, with the exception of the bathroom shelves which make it somewhat awkward to shave, Inch is delightful.

- ● **OPEN:** All year except Xmas.
Dinner to non residents 7.30pm-9.30pm.
- ● **ROOMS:** Five rooms, all en suite.
- ● **AVERAGE PRICE:**
£20 per person sharing, £25 single.
Dinner £25.
No Service Charge.
- ● **CREDIT CARDS:**) Visa, Access/Master.

- ● **NOTES:**
Full Licence.
No Wheelchair Access.
Children – cots, babysitting.
No Pets in house.
From Thurles, take the road at the top right hand side of the square, marked "Other Routes".
Drive for four miles.
A sign says "Welcome To The Rag".
Inch House is signposted 200 yrds further along on the left.

BUGGY'S GLENCAIRN INN ◈

Ken & Cathleen Buggy
Glencairn
Co Waterford
Tel: (058) 56232

"Everybody in Ireland is busy exporting the idea of the Irish bar throughout the world", says Ken Buggy. "So, I decided to open an English inn in Ireland".

How inimitable is the droll, hilarious humour of Ken Buggy. Many will have wondered where Ken and Cathleen went to after they sold The Old Presbytery, in Kinsale. The answer is that they came here, close to Lismore, in the sweeping plains of Waterford after you descend down from the Vee, to a fine old house of elegant proportions which they have – you expected this – restored to immaculate order.

The bar does look somewhat like an old inn, but it looks like an old inn designed by Ken Buggy. That familiar pell-mell perfection, that air of abandoned contrivance, which made the Presbytery so inimitable is back in action, and Buggy's Glencairn Inn is tribute and testament to some people's ability to place the right thing in the right place.

It achieves just the right effect; you want to sit down in front of the fire and drink a brace of pints and a tray full of whiskeys, chat away for the whole evening. If you hate the way modern pubs are so streamlined and self-conscious, then Buggy's is for you.

The other good news is that there are now two rooms, finished in Ken's inimitable style in which to stay over the pub, and he has begun to serve bar food at lunch and dinner.

● **OPEN:** Bar food 12.30pm-2pm, 6pm-9pm Mon-Sun.
● **ROOMS:** Two rooms, both en suite.
● **AVERAGE PRICE:**
B&B £20 per person sharing.
Bar food under £5. No Service Charge.
● **CREDIT CARDS:** No credit cards.

● **NOTES:**
Full Licence.
Wheelchair Access in bar, not rooms.
Children – young children welcome up to 6.30pm.
Take the Tallow road from Lismore, turn right at the garage from where Glencairn is signposted. Buggy's is in the centre of the village.

CARRIGAHILLA HOUSE & GARDENS ◈

Vincent & Margaret Morrissey
Stradbally, Co Waterford
Tel & Fax: (051) 293127

The simplicity and calmness of Carrigahilla is delightful, and the house retains much of the air of the former convent it once was. Margaret and Vincent attend to both inside and out: the gardens, designed by Margaret, are cleverly inter-linked, connecting the different themes of Secret Shady garden, Herb Garden, Fruit and vegetable Parterre, Woodland and Cottage garden, and so on.

Inside, meanwhile, the discipline of this couple is fully evident in their cooking, which makes full use of the garden's herbs – mushroom and thyme leaf tart; purée of onion soup with garden herbs – and also shows the dedication to getting the obvious things correct, inspired by a Ballymaloe course – perfect beurre blanc with poached salmon; excellent mayonnaise with rosettes of smoked salmon, delectable salad leaves from the garden and flavour-packed vegetables, which again only have to be dug up and carried in from the vegetable garden.

This patience and perfectionism is charming, and the food is well matched by smashing wines from David Dennison's excellent Wine Vault, in Waterford.

● **OPEN:** Noon-2.30pm,
6pm-10pm Mon-Sat.
(Open all afternoon in the summer).
● **AVERAGE PRICE:**
B&B £20-£25 per person sharing.
Dinner £22.50. No Service Charge.
● **CREDIT CARDS:** Visa, Access/Master.

● **OPEN:**
Wine Licence.
Children – welcome, cots, high chair.
Wheelchair Access – to restaurant, not rooms.
Signposted from Stradbally.

DWYER'S OF MARY STREET ◎
Martin Dwyer
5 Mary Street, Waterford
Co Waterford
Tel: (051) 77478

Martin Dwyer likes to cook, enjoys the business of cooking for people, and it shows.

His food is very pleasing to eat, thanks to interesting and considered variations in texture and colour, and clever relocations with certain ingredients

Lettuce and sorrel soup is a fine signature dish, and that sorrel can turn up again in an onion sauce to partner local salmon.

His fish cooking is very strong, and he will accentuate the rich taste of monkfish by wrapping it in a herb crust and serving it with tapenade.

Garlic prawns in a rosti nest – a smart rejigging of something that might be more usually found at home in a Chinese restaurant – is another signature dish of a cook who comfortably walks that line between food which maintains his own interest – by virtue of presenting himself with a changing culinary challenge, and by continually introducing new foods and new tastes – and who can manage to make this food seem comforting and accessible to a somewhat cautious clientele.

But not too cautious, a clientele, it should be said. Mr Dwyer has built a devoted following in Waterford since moving here.

Mr Dwyer has built this rapport with his audience by slowly bringing them along with him as he has matured and developed as a cook,. He has gradually gotten them more involved in the evolution of Dwyer's, has managed to make them eager for more exciting dishes.

At the same time, cleverly, he has always maintained those twin pillars of his style of cooking, a style dedicated to presenting food which is both considerate and honest.

The restaurant itself is a molly-coddling sort of space, tucked away in a quiet street not too far from the waterfont.

Good service and a good wine list has helped his impressive championing of serious food in the town, and the combination of an almost-maternal care, soft music and good food is quite charming.

● **OPEN:** 6pm-10pm Mon-Sat.
● **AVERAGE PRICE:**
Dinner £20 (£14 "early bird").
No Service Charge.
● **CREDIT CARDS:**
Visa, Access/Master, Amex, Diners.

● **NOTES:**
Restaurant Licence.
Wheelchair Access.
Children – half portions.
Waterford town centre, 200yds south of the bridge.

HANORA'S COTTAGE ◈

Eoin Wall
Nire Valley
Clonmel
Co Waterford
Tel: (052) 36134
Fax: (052) 25145

The world is full of golfers whose lack of skill is not something they wish to be reminded of.

It would not please them, then, as they lie awake at night worrying about their handicap of 24, and dreaming about the happy day when they can get it down to 22, to know that Seamus Wall has a golf handicap of 2.

That is correct.

Two.

But golfers – competitive souls that they are – should not dismiss Hanora's Cottage, the Wall family's B&B in the Nire Valley, north of Ballymacarbry, just because their golfing inadequacies will be accentuated.

Pretend, instead, when you arrive, that you have never held a club, never worn a pair of checked socks and a lemon-yellow sweater.

Simply turn up at Hanora's and declare: "I am here for the hill-walking. And I have never met Fred Couples. I have never even met Fred Singles".

They will understand.

Snuggled within the silent embrace of one of the Comeragh mountain valleys, Hanora's Cottage overlooks the river Nire and is overlooked itself by the Nire church, set slightly higher at the foot of the mountains.

Many folk come here to partake of hill-walking with Seamus, but another attraction is the fact that Seamus and Mary's son Eoin – a Ballymaloe School trained chef – carefully sources good foods for the breakfasts and dinners that add the final touch of quietude to this quiet place.

Breakfast bacon comes from the Rudds in County Offaly, while local organic grower Vicky Heslop supplies him with vegetables.

Don't worry about eating all of that huge breakfast, by the way, for a brace of miles over the Comeragh Mountains will get rid of it all.

And perhaps, as you scale the hills, it is the right time to reflect on Mark Twain's sage statement, that golf is nothing more than a good walk spoiled.

● **OPEN:** All year except Xmas.
Dinner from 7.30pm.
● **ROOMS:** Eight rooms, all en suite,
one with jacuzzi.
● **AVERAGE PRICE:** B&B £22.50-£25
per person sharing, £35 single.
Dinner £17.50.
● **CREDIT CARDS:**
Visa, Access/Master, Amex, Diners.

● **NOTES:**
Wine Licence.
No Wheelchair Access.
Children – welcome. No pets.
Turn off the Clonmel/Dungarvan road at
Ballymacarbry. The house is four miles
down the road, beside the Nire church.

McCLUSKEY'S ⊚
Paul McCluskey
High Street, Waterford
Co Waterford
Tel: (051) 57766

Paul McCluskey cooked with distinction in Waterford Castle when he had tenure of the kitchen in that grand old pile.

He has now moved into town, to a much leaner, simpler and more modern space than the gentle, bourgeois grace of the castle.

But, in truth, the move is a good one, for his food has always been modern and expertly achieved, a very personal style whose search for simplicity was somewhat at odds with the old-fashioned style of the castle.

What is especially pleasing, and perhaps surprising, about this modernism, is the fact that Mr McCluskey has been behind a stove for a good many years now.

But his style has not been blunted at all, perhaps because he has never ceased to experiment, has never ceased to enjoy the creative side of the kitchen. Long before anyone treated vegetarian cookery with any sort of seriousness, for example Paul McCluskey was preparing fine, considered vegetarian dishes.

McCluskey's shows that very true, respectful style at full tilt: tagliatelle with salmon, Dunmore plaice with a red pepper and pecan pesto; Moroccan braised beef with couscous.

Prices are very, very keen, for it is Mr McCluskey's determination to make his restaurant not only approachable, but affordable. It is a laudable aim, and one which he seems set to achieve, with gas in the tank.

Certainly, this is the sort of food you could eat every day of the week. In summertime, they plan to have tables outside on the pedestrian area, so let's pray for fine weather.

● **OPEN:** Noon-2.30pm, 6pm-10pm Mon-
Sat. (Open all afternoon in the summer).
● **AVERAGE PRICE:** Table d'hôte Lunch
under £7.50-£9.50. À la carte Dinner
under £20. No Service Charge.
● **CREDIT CARDS:** Visa, Access/Master.

● **NOTES:**
Wine Licence.
Wheelchair Access. Children – welcome.
Recommended for vegetarians.
In the centre of Waterford.

ULSTER

breaking
for
the
border

MACNEAN BISTRO ⓇⒶ
Nevan Maguire
Blacklion, Co Cavan
Tel: (072) 53022

Sometimes, you wonder just what the ordinary, decent, culinarily cautious folk of Cavan must think of young Nevan Maguire.

His thrilling skills not only offer the most subversively delicious food in the county, with twists and turns offered with just about every staple you can think of – pan fried lamb with a black pudding mousse; fillet of turbot on a seafood risotto – but he has slowly been introducing outrageous ingredients such as bison, alligator and ostrich to the menu of the MacNean.

Mr Maguire loves the dazzle of fashionably decorated plates, loves the convolution of spun sugar hats on desserts, the luxuriance of rich chocolate puddings, the ethereality of mousses built from black pudding.

Puddings and deserts are perhaps his greatest speciality, and he has a knack of winning very serious cheffy competitions with his awesome inventions. This is someplace to make sure you save yourself for dessert, for Mr Maguire is one of the country's finest patissiers.

But he is sage, at the same time, and local game is carefully sourced, and offered on a series of seasonal menus, fish dishes are restricted to what can be purchased fresh, and local organic vegetables are impeccably flavoursome. This is a kitchen that cares about what it sends out, each and every time.

For a young man, he shows a thoroughly mature understanding of what a restaurant needs to offer in order to succeed.

But maybe the reason why he is so sage is because he is the only the younger generation of Maguire to be involved in the kitchen at the MacNean.

Nevan's mother, Vera, offers some counterbalance to this youthful brilliance, and the Bistro menus continue to offer relatively simple dishes alongside this young man's flights of fancy.

You can get a fine sirloin here with a potato gratin, breads are excellent, Sunday lunch offers all the traditional fare one would expect of a country restaurant.

But, when you step into the MacNean, you should abandon caution to the wind. For it is the flights of fancy which should drag you to Blacklion, and Mr Maguire is a very happening culinary talent. Do note there are now also rooms.

● **OPEN:**
5.30pm-9pm Tue-Sat, 12.30pm-9pm Sun.
● **ROOMS:** Ten rooms, all en suite.
● **AVERAGE PRICE:** Table d'hôte Sun Lunch £12. Table d'hôte Dinner £22. No Service Charge.
● **CREDIT CARDS:** Visa, Access/Master.

● **NOTES:**
Wine Licence.
Children – welcome. Indoor playroom. Children eight yrs free accommodation in parent's room. Early evening meal on request.
Early Bird menu, 5.30pm-7pm, £12.
Two sittings for Sun lunch, 12.30pm & 3pm.
On the main street in Blacklion.

ARDNAMONA HOUSE & GARDENS ◬

Amabel & Kieran Clarke
Lough Eske
Co Donegal
Tel: (073) 22650, Fax: (073) 22819

List the locations in Ireland which afford you heart-stopping beauty – the Beara Peninsula on a fine day, north Donegal on a wild day, sunset over the River Liffey in Dublin, Connemara in early autumn – and you will find that there is nowhere, but nowhere, that can compare to Lough Eske.

This is an impossibly beautiful place. Walk down the stairs in Ardnamona in the morning, stroll to the front windows and, like some dubious Romantic poet in a dubious Hollywood movie, you almost have to cry out "Be still, my heart!", for the perfection of nature which you will see before you seems all too good to be true.

The stillness, the concentrated surfeit of water and wood as the Blue Stack mountains cradle the eager waters of Lough Eske, is unforgettable.

Amabel and Kieran Clarke's house sits fast in the wrap of lough and forest, and the bloom of rich summer greens and blues is matched by the shocking russet vividness of the ferns in the winter. There are five rooms in the house, south facing, brightly pastelly, their modest design perfectly judged and effected.

Mrs Clarke is a confident cook, which means that her food is simple – roast quail on toast, good roasted lamb, splendid gratins of courgette and other seasonal vegetables, excellent potatoes – the perfect dinner in the perfect house.

Mr Clarke has one of those droll, quiet, impish senses of humour which are so proudly a facet of the Donegal character. It can take a little time to prise this sardonic, funny side of him but, when you do, he is cracking good company.

In the hands of anybody else, Ardnamona might well wind up like some sort of stuffed architectural and botanical peacock, for the house also has one of the oldest collections of tree rhododendrons in Ireland, but Kieran and Amabel puncture any sort of stuffiness with their calm, democratic spirits.

● **OPEN:** All year except Xmas and New Year.
● **ROOMS:** Five rooms, two en suite, three with private bathrooms.
● **AVERAGE PRICE:**
£35-£45 per person sharing.
Set Dinner £17.
No Service Charge.
● **CREDIT CARDS:**
Visa, Access/Master.

● **NOTES:**
Advance booking essential.
Dinner, 8.30pm, for guests only, if pre-booked by noon.
Wine Licence.
No Wheelchair Access.
Children – high chairs, cots, babysitting.
Dogs allowed, but not in bedrooms.
Leave Donegal town on the N15 towards Letterkenny. After 5kms take a small turning on the left marked "Harvey's Point". Carry straight on for 6kms; the white gates for Ardnamona are marked on the right.

CASTLEMURRAY HOUSE ○○
Thierry Delcros
Dunkineely
Co Donegal
Tel: (073) 37022

Thierry Delcros is such a good cook that you could run the risk of taking his expertise for granted.

His style is so subtle and skillful that he can produce food which seems to speak of pure culinary logic, and it is so deliciously persuasive that, as you eat it, you can't imagine that anyone would ever do things differently from the way this spirited, sparky chef does them.

He is a true Donegal cook, for a Frenchman, in that his style owes nothing to fashion and is embedded in the true flavours and tastes of the countryside.

He does what he does, and he does it startlingly well, creating cooking that emerges from cuisine paysanne and cuisine bourgeois to take on its own mantle.

His cooking is truly complete, the result of a solid education which allows his creations to seem effortless. But the lack of tension in his work owes as much to the fact that he has no nonsensical ego getting in the way: the man is a professional, simple as that.

That professionalism is memorably expressed in classical dishes: onion soup; duck pâté salad; prawns with garlic butter; fillet of beef with wild mushrooms; sole with lemon butter; crispy lobster.

The lack of ornamentation in his style allows M. Delcros to deliver the tastes of his ingredients directly, making these classics vibrant and rich, satisfying and provocative to the appetite.

The dining room in Castlemurray House, with its jaw-dropping views across the bay, is the perfect place in which to savour this food, for it enjoys the same simplicity, and luxuriance in the elements which you find in the cooking.

For many regulars, the trip is completed by staying overnight in the affordable, cosy bedrooms. But don't imagine that you are going to an hotel: this is a restaurant with rooms, so you carry your own bags and there is no room service.

But that actually suits the straightforward, very honest nature of the house and the kitchen. Castlemurray is an unpretentious place and, like everyone else, you are here for fun, maybe spending an eternity over Sunday lunch – it lasts all afternoon – or getting coochy, smoochy over dinner for two.

● **OPEN:** 7pm-9.30pm Mon-Sun ('till 10pm Sat and Sun). (Closed Mon-Wed off season).
● **ROOMS:** Ten, all en suite.
● **AVERAGE PRICE:** B&B £26. Table d'hôte Dinner over £17-£23. No Service Charge.
● **CREDIT CARDS:** Visa, Access/Master.

● **NOTES:**
Full Licence.
Children – welcome, high chairs, cots.
Castlemurray is signposted just after the village of Dunkineely, on the N56 road west from Donegal to Bruckless and Killybegs.

HILTON PARK ⚫❖
Johnny & Lucy Madden
Scotshouse
Co Monaghan
Tel: (047) 56007
Fax: (047) 56033

It is an indicator of the intellectual resonance which Lucy Madden brings to her work that the food book on which she has been slowly working for several years now should be an exhaustive study of both the potato and recipes for using the humble spud. This autodidactic approach is typical of her work, and gives a clue to the charm, and strength, of Hilton Park.

For this is perhaps the most experimental of the country houses, albeit that such an idea might seem absurd. But Hilton is almost a template of what the country house could be, and can be, and should be. Where other houses appear to have simply fallen together and to act as a warehouse for old furniture and old ideas, this is a house where the owners seem clearly to have considered the very idea itself of the country house existing at the end of the twentieth century, have re-assessed the idea of country house cooking, and thought about the idea of country house hospitality.

Indeed, this analysis of what country house cooking can be is vital. Mrs Madden's imprimatur is to avoid the dewy-eyed, Beetonesque brouhaha which some think appropriate to the country house. Instead, the basis of her cooking lies in the very relationship between farming and eating.

And, then, their produce is put at the service of Mrs Madden's intricate, considered cooking, cooking where the vibrant energy of these foods is assessed and then simply released. Once again, the backbone of the food here is the fact of the careful consideration and analysis it enjoys, and the result is food which is expressive and truly delicious.

But don't imagine that this experiment is arid or unfeeling, that Hilton Park is some sort of Bauhaus Country House. It is not, and the cleverality of the Maddens makes it a seductive place, a canvas of pleasure.

Unlike other places, Hilton doesn't allow itself to wallow in the embrace of its considerable history. It is not a nostalgic house, a joint where you are invited to trip out for a few days into some moribund idea of "gracious living". It is gracious, certainly, but the tactility at work in the furnishings, in the bold use of colour and objects, and the wit of both Johnny and Lucy, make it a very real, living space.

- **OPEN:** Mar-Oct.
- **ROOMS:** Five rooms, all en suite.
- **AVERAGE PRICE:**
  B&B £55 per person sharing.
  Set Dinner £25. No Service Charge.
- **CARDS:** Visa, Access/Master.

- **NOTES:**
  Wine Licence.
  Children – by arrangement only.
  No pets.
  Three miles out of Clones on the road to Ballyhaise, the entrance gates are dark green with silver falcons.

NORTHERN IRELAND

the gold coast

and the glenshane pass

MADDYBENNY FARM HOUSE ◈
Rosemary White
18 Maddybenny Park
Portrush
Co Antrim
Tel: (01265) 823394

Rosemary White's breakfast presents a drama of multiple choice. And when we say drama, we mean drama. We mean the breakfast equivalent of the Ring Cycle. We are talking something as extensive as "Heimat" by Edgar Reitz or Terry Riley's "Salome Dances for Peace".

Breakfast in Maddybenny is not so much "The Remembrance of Things Past", but "The Contemplation of Things to Come".

First of all, the porridge. You can have it your way or The Maddybenny Way. The Maddybenny Way is to serve the grains with runny honey, either Drambuie or Irish Mist, and lashings of cream.

You'll have it The Maddybenny Way.

Then, the agony of decision continues. Which main dish will it be? The Ulster Fry, with good old Ulster soda and fadge? Kipper fillets poached in lemon juice and dill?

Trout braised in lemon butter, then served with smoked bacon and mushrooms? Maybe a smoked haddock ramekin? Or lamb's kidneys? Boiled eggs? Scrambled eggs?

On and on the drama unfolds.

You could flunk the responsibility, of course, and just content yourself with the fresh soda bread and toast, the handmade jams and marm-alades, the country butter, a clatter of cups of Earl Grey, or maybe some hot chocolate.

But, you aren't going to do that. You are going to grab the bull by the horns, grab the main role, be the main player in the drama.

At the end of the whole delicious thing, you will secretly applaud yourself.

In every other way, Mrs White will make life easy for you, helpfully arranging bookings in local restaurants, explaining all and sundry about all and sundry which could possibly be of interest locally and, if you are brave enough, you can hack out with a pony from their riding centre.

There are new self-catering apartments on the farm, but you would be more than crazy to miss out on the drama of breakfast.

- **OPEN:** All year.
- **ROOMS:**
Three rooms, all en suite.
- **AVERAGE PRICE:**
£20-£25 per person sharing.
No Service Charge.
- **CREDIT CARDS:**
Visa, Access/Master.

- **NOTES:**
No restaurant, but reservations made locally.
No Licence.
No Wheelchair Access.
Children – 30% off, high chairs, cots.
Pets accommodated in outside stables.
Maddybenny Riding Centre is signposted off the A29 road which runs between Coleraine and Portrush.

NICK'S WAREHOUSE ◎⊖
Nick & Kathy Price
35/39 Hill Street
Belfast BT1
Co Antrim
Tel: (01232) 439690

Nick's Warehouse is built on a foundation of fun, good humour and an altogether awesome amiability which you will not find anywhere else in the country. If restaurants are built in the image of their owners then we can say that the Warehouse is unpretentious, enjoys a joke, like a drink, and has an appreciation of how to conjure up the pleasures of food and wine which is simply instinctive.

Lots of other places in Ireland are like the Warehouse, but they don't have what it has. It's unique. Especially on a Friday lunchtime. Friday lunch in here feels like a meeting of the End Is Nigh Club, called by the executive committee just after they've got some hot news about how nigh is nigh.

What underpins the foundation of the Warehouse is a streetwise, sassy style of cooking, combined with a streetwise, sassy style of service that bears all the hallmarks of the Price's quiet extrovertism, and you always get more than you bargained for.

The lack of pretension and artifice might lead you to believe that it is a straightforward, everyday sort of place, but it is no such thing. The thought and care evident in the service, the wine list, the selection of beers and, finally, in the cooking, is much better than one has a right to expect from such a busy place. Just

because they don't put on airs and graces, you should not lose sight of the fact that the cooking here is very clever, very well achieved, and sublimely delightful.

Like many modern cooks, Mr Price is a magpie, filching, foraging and finding ideas and influences from books and cooks, from cultures and countries. He has a very true hand with the eastern spicing he likes so much – a sharp chilli and soy dressing gives oomph! to a dish of monkfish and crab, whilst sesame seed and ginger will be used with an avocado and smoked chicken salad.

But in truth he remains a classicist, albeit a multicultural one, and dishes such as salmon with a dill butter sauce, or a wonderful calves' liver with shallots and balsamic vinegar, are solid senders of good flavours, their combinations embedded in a very true concept of cooking.

The wine list is not only smashing, it is the most amusing list in the country. Altogether, the Warehouse is some sort of super place.

● **OPEN:** 11.30pm-11pm Mon-Sat.
Closed Mon evening.
Lunch served noon-3pm, dinner 6pm-9pm.
● **AVERAGE PRICE:** Wine Bar Lunch under £10. Table d'hôte Dinner £17.50.
No Service Charge.
● **CREDIT CARDS:**
Visa, Access/Master, Amex.

● **NOTES:**
Credit card purchases under £10 incur a 50p surcharge.
Full Licence.
Children – welcome upstairs only.
Recommended for Vegetarians.
Hill Street is near the University of Ulster.

RAMORE ®
George McAlpin
The Harbour
Portrush
Co Antrim
Tel: (01265) 824313

It has been the most marvellous fun, not to mention the most delicious fun, to see how The Ramore has altered its character over the last couple of years, and become a simpler, more democratic and much funkier place.

The re-invention began with the creation of a more informal dining space, with the kitchen becoming fully open to view ,and a set of bar chairs established at the counter.

The paraphernalia of a working kitchen – the brigade of whisks, the tumbling tresses of garlic, the bottles of oil, the dog-eared texts – are all on happy exhibition, along with their white-clad employers, who intersect with one another with the sure-footedness of dancers.

It's a charming entertainment, as you sip aperitifs and nibble bread, but when the food arrives, it is quickly, strictly, heads-down.

For in parallel with the design renovation, George McAlpin's cooking has shifted its concentration away from a convoluted French style, and has brought on board the lighter influences of the Pacific Rim.

Thus, whilst we find the signatures of foreign influence – tempura prawns with diced peppers under a trio of Mexican tostados; tagliatelle with a slurpy Roquefort sauce; char-grilled chicken with the sweetness of sun-dried tomatoes for annotation –

it is just as much fun to stick with George's revisions of classic dishes, for they reveal a great sense of humour.

You can eat prawn cocktail and then steak and chips with fried onion rings here, and it will be a belter of a meal: the cocktail suffuse with perfect ingredients, the steak served with onion rings so crisp and light they could be called tempura, the chips pure magic.

Chicken and duck liver parfait has a column of melba toast stored high in the style of railway sleepers, whilst exquisitely fresh fish is balanced atop a tower of perfect chips in a dazzling architectural tumbril. Funky food, fun food.

The staff are super-duper and extra patient – we're afraid that it was our party which stayed 'till three a.m – the wine list short and clever – house wines are very good here – and the whole organisation devoted to delivering the best of the best times.

Do note that there is a wine bar downstairs which is even less formal, and which is ideal for lunches and snacks during the day.

● **OPEN:** Open 6.30pm-10.30pm Tue-Sat (downstairs wine bar opens for lunch).
● **AVERAGE PRICE:** Dinner £20.
No Service Charge.
● **CREDIT CARDS:** Visa, Access/Master.

● **NOTES:**
Full Licence.
Children – controlled children welcome.
Right on the harbour in Portrush, as far down the one-way system as you can drive.

ROSCOFF ◐✪

Paul & Jeanne Rankin
7 Lesley Hse, Shaftesbury Square
Belfast BT2, Co Antrim
Tel: (01232) 331532

Despite their well documented successes in the field of television and with their excellent cookery books, Paul and Jeanne Rankin, first and foremost, are cooks and restaurateurs, and they have remained as dedicated and devoted to their craft as they have ever been.

Indeed, apart from a brief, glorious period in the early days of the restaurant, when a quartet of Paul Rankin, Robbie Millar, Eugene Callaghan and Noel McMeel were actually sweating behind these stoves together, Roscoff has perhaps never produced better food than it is currently doing.

The stupendous quality of the cooking can be explained by the fact that the Rankins have continued to allow their cooking to evolve intellectually.

Where others try to hit on a successful groove and then milk it for all it is worth, the Rankins have permitted their ideas on food to mature, and have moved their thinking on how it should be cooked and served to higher ground.

The style of menu now – no set dinner, no a la carte, just a panoply of starters, main courses and desserts at a fixed price – has allowed Mr Rankin to pursue his idea of integral, essentially flavoured cooking to a greater degree.

In addition to this achievement of unadorned tastes, the food has also become less serious: they are not trying to impress anyone by pyrotechnics or sleight of hand.

And so, what does impress is the articulation and precision of flavour. Seared beef salad with Chinese mustard greens produces a welter of pepper and mustard flavours between the ingredients; the chilli cream underneath some crab cakes stores a little shock of heat to counter the sweet flakes of shellfish.

Salmon on a sauce of potato and basil is perfect, the potato trickled out with fish stock, little oven-dried tomatoes giving a contrast of colour, and other main courses show a search for the perfect affinity between ingredients which is imitative of Chinese cooking: creamed lentils and coriander with fillets of sole; duck with roast garlic, thyme and black pepper; lamb with rosemary and creamed pumpkin.

Desserts in Roscoff have always been sublime, and pumpkin tart with a creme anglaise shows just how dare-to-be-simple the place can be: a piece of tart and a custard, both perfect, and needing absolutely nothing else.

The peril of their media stardom, of course, lies in the fact that other work drags the Rankins away from the stove, and no one can doubt that Roscoff works best when they are there in the kitchen.

But their importance remains simply that the revolt into coolness which has so revolutionised eating in the North in recent years was begun with Roscoff and, today, it remains the trailblazer.

● **OPEN:** 12.15pm-2.15pm Mon-Fri, 6.30pm-10.30pm Mon-Sat.

● **AVERAGE PRICE:**
Table d'hôte Lunch £15.50.
Table d'hôte Dinner £24.95.
● **CREDIT CARDS:**
Visa, Access/Master, Amex.

● **NOTES:**
Full Licence.
Children – welcome.
Recommended for Vegetarians.
Belfast City centre.

SUN KEE ®⊖
Edmund Lau
38 Donegal Pass
Belfast BT7
Co Antrim
Tel: (01232) 312016

Think of every cliché you know about Chinese restaurants: indifferent food, which is totally inauthentic; tacky decor; which is totally inauthentic, brushque service, which is totally authentic and, at the end of it all, the sort of bill which causes severe bruising to the credit card.

Now take yourself and the family off to the Sun Kee, just off Shartesbury Square in the heart of the city. Push through the pair of doors, and there, in all its modest glory, is a little four-square, mirror-walled room. There are a couple of doors at the bottom end, there is a little counter over on your left, and in between is a collection of tables, with a television set over against the wall oozing some sport or whatnot.

Perfect.

The Sun Kee is the real thing, and a reminder that the interiors of Chinese restaurants do not need to look like they have been kitted out from a car boot sale of lacquered panels.

Unadorned, uncompromised, Edmund Lau's Sun Kee is the friendliest Chinese restaurant in the country, and its simple, true food is awesome.

Their speciality is hot pot dishes: monkfish and char sui offers the delectable, sympathetic flavours of the battered fish and the thin slices of pork along with choi sum, baby corn, carrots, spring onions and Chinese mushrooms; beef flank hot pot has beef, potatoes and baby turnips in a slurpsome sauce, but anything amongst their speciality dishes – don't miss the roast duck – is zingy with freshness and in-your-face-tastes.

The hot and sour soups are terrific, the beef or the prawns with salt and chilli are glorious, and they do the sort of noodles which your kids can't stop eating.

It is also cheap, a thrill which is further helped by the fact that they allow you to bring your own booze. Your dining companions, for the most part, will be members of Belfast's Chinese community, all having as good a time as you are.

● **OPEN:** 5pm-1pm Sun-Thur,
5pm-11.30pm Sat. Closed Fri.
● **AVERAGE PRICE:** Meals around £12.
No Service Charge.
● **CREDIT CARDS:**
No Credit Cards.

● **NOTES:**
No Licence, Bring Your Own Wine.
Children – welcome.
Belfast City centre. Donegal Pass runs off
Shartesbury Square.

DEANE'S ON THE SQUARE ®
Michael Deane
Station Square
Helen's Bay
Co Down
Tel: (01247) 852841/273155

Michael Deane is a dazzlingly fine cook, and a man devoted to the business of being a chef. Indeed, his work can oftentimes seem like a map of current obsessions and attractions within the business of cooking, with his talent allowing him to select whatever fashions he chooses, and make them work.

A menu might offer a dish of tatin of lamb with mushy peas, alongside Thai style breast of duck wonton, and both will be textbook successes. Indeed, not only will they be successfully achieved, but they will also be humourous, friendly, and hugely enjoyable.

If you love the business of dissecting influences in food, and seeing how someone with copious skill reinterprets them according to his own métier, then Mr Deane is an entertainment of operatic proportions.

He does great things such as lemon tart, and onion rings, and gravadlax, and bacon mash in the shape of a cottage loaf, and he does them all perfectly, which proves that he is a patient, as well as a perfect-ionist, cook.

He is able to identify and extract flavours with great precision, so dinner can offer a sumptuous assortment of true tastes: fillet of salmon with saffron; a clear soup of chicken and lemongrass; sinuous beef fillet.

So why, then, isn't Deane's decked with stars and accolades? Why does it remain something of a well-kept secret? The answer lies in the fact that Mr Deane's brilliance is not matched by his waiting staff, who seem diffident, nervous, ever eager to avoid eye-contact. This is a shame, for this kitchen produces food that is brassy and bold, and all he needs is a bustling, bistro buzz going on outside to truly achieve his enormous potential.

One good person to knock his troupe into shape will do the job, one good person to make sure the tape machine gets changed and to check that everything is all right, to source a better wine list, and then the honours Mr Deane deserves and craves will beat a path to his door.

He will get there, for sure, and he deserves to, for this is a gifted, individual chef with a style that is all his own. We look forward to the day when Mr Deane's accessible, enjoyable food finds the atmosphere in which it will flourish.

● **OPEN:** 7pm-10pm Tue-Sat.
12.30pm-2.30pm Sun.
● **AVERAGE PRICE:**
Dinner £19-£23.75. Sun Lunch £16.50,
Dinner £24.95. No Service Charge.
● **CREDIT CARDS:**
Visa, Access/Master, Amex, Diners.

● **NOTES:**
Full Licence.
Children – welcome.
The restaurant overlooks the station platform in Helen's Bay.
Look for the newly-restored tower.

SHANKS ⓡ ✪
Richard Gibson
Robbie & Shirley Millar
The Blackwood, Crawfordsburn
Road, nr Bangor, Co Down
Tel: (01247) 853313

Robbie Millar's cooking works a seam all his own, drawing in ideas with a freshness of conception that makes his work very special.

His background was fairly conventional – but where he has stepped out of the mainframe has been with a year spent in Corfu, and a further year when he and his wife Shirley travelled around Europe in a camper van, eating as they went.

"You learn more from eating out than you do from working in a kitchen", Millar has said – and this travelling has graced his style with an expansiveness which is thrilling.

Take one of his signature dishes: seared scallops, avocado frittata and a charred tomato salsa. You look at this seemingly irreconcilable array of ingredients – the sweet scallops, the oily avocado, the toasty tomatoes, the surprise of the cooked egg – and, for the life of you, you reckon it can't work, that there are no obvious sympathies between the flavours.

Yet Millar can not only make this work, he turns it into a masterpiece.

If there are consistent themes found in his work, then it may be the fact that he utilises a sweetness in his cooking which makes it friendly and approachable.

He uses pesto and Parmesan shavings to ally with a dish of potato gnocchi and chicken livers, encourages the sweet interplay of mushroom polenta with squab, or pumpkin ravioli with a tomato and sage butter, or an apple mash with venison, or a sun-dried tomato aioli with hake. This is food that you can't help falling in love with, and any intellectual doubts about its unlikeliness are swept away the very second you taste this cooking.

He works his magic in Shanks, a lean, cool place where Shirley Millar shows the sort of skills at front of house which you can only be born with. The design goes against the grain of Northern Ireland suburban – but Shanks has proven to be a huge success.

Partly this is also due to the skills of the decisively enigmatic Richard Gibson, the general manager of the complex, and these three together are are some sort of dream team. The challenge of unlikeliness is what drives them, the challenge of showing that you can tie up all these disparate elements and dissolve any perceived tensions between them.

It is a mighty achievement.

● **OPEN:** Restaurant – 12.30pm-2.30pm, 7pm-10pm Tue-Sat.
Closed lunch Sat, & all Sun & Mon.
Bar snacks 12.30pm-2pm Tue-Fri & Sun.
● **AVERAGE PRICE:** Lunch £14.95.
Dinner £24.95. No Service Charge.
● **CARDS:** Visa, Access/Master.

● **NOTES:**
Full Licence.
Children – welcome.
On the main Belfast/Bangor dual carriageway, take the turning for Newtownards, follow directions to Ards, then look for the signs.

BEECH HILL ⓞⓟⓢ✪
Country House Hotel
Seamus Donnelly
32 Ardmore Road, nr Derry
Co Londonderry
Tel: (01504) 49279,
Fax: (01504) 45366

"Simplicity means taking raw food, understanding it and cooking it very little", says Noel McMeel. "You cook food to keep the flavours, for the flavours are all there".

He has always been a terrific cook, but the lack of tension and artifice in his work now, its obdurate correctness and sympathy, is sublime. "You work with what is around you, and you use the skills of your suppliers to make a good act, but you must distinguish the ingredients, you must find what things are good with what".

In practice, McMeel's interpretation of this diktat is devastatingly true. With a dish such as grouse lasagne, the leaves of pasta cleverly interleaved with spinach, the flavours are soft and flowing, with a touch of coriander used both to cut any suggestion of richness and to add counterpoint.

A nage of seafood allies white beans with lemon balm and an array of fish and shellfish, whilst chicken finds the perfect match with a banana bread stuffing.

This feel for unity amongst ingredients extends right through to McMeel's sympathy for colour: a basil sauce to showcase a terrine of salmon; a brilliantly tricolor pasta terrine, the warm glow of a marvellous soda bread with saffron and raisins. At all times, McMeel's skills are at the service of his ingredients. Where so much modern food tends to the pretentious and winds up tasting tortured, his work is blissfully erudite and pronounced, cooking which is truly logical.

The young patissier Gordon Smith is able to conjure desserts almost as ethereal as his boss's cooking – the chocolate tower is a dream, the crème brûlée with coconut a riot – and thus concludes an adventure of dignified and complete cooking. For such fine food, the wine list deserves to be better, and is one feature which deserves attention.

If Noel McMeel was the Beech Hill's only calling card, they would be doing well, but he is fortunate to enjoy the support of a terrific staff, with Crawford, the manager, and Michelle, the receptionist, as creative and inspiring as their chef. The rooms in the hotel are comfortable, but best of all there is a feeling of an age-old hospitality and care about the Beech Hill.

● **OPEN:** All year. 7am-10am, 12.30pm-2.30pm, 6.30pm-10pm Mon-Sun.
● **ROOMS:** Seventeen rooms, all en suite.
● **AVERAGE PRICE:**
Table d'hôte Lunch £13.95.
Table d'hôte Dinner £20.95.
No Service Charge.
● **CREDIT CARDS:**
Visa, Access/Master, Amex.

● **NOTES:**
Full Licence. Limited Wheelchair Access.
Recommended for Vegetarians.
Beech Hill is signposted from the A2, just past Drumahoe as you come into Derry on the main Belfast road.

INDEX

OTHER TITLES FROM ESTRAGON PRESS

WRITTEN BY
JOHN & SALLY McKENNA

THE BRIDGESTONE IRISH FOOD GUIDE

THE BRIDGESTONE VEGETARIANS' GUIDE TO IRELAND

THE BRIDGESTONE 100 BEST SERIES:

THE BRIDGESTONE 100 BEST RESTAURANTS IN IRELAND

THE BRIDGESTONE 100 BEST PLACES TO STAY IN IRELAND

THE BRIDGESTONE 100 BEST PLACES TO EAT IN DUBLIN

**THE BRIDGESTONE TITLES ARE AVAILABLE
FROM ALL GOOD BOOK SHOPS**

NOTES